Wild, Wild World of Animals

Dangerous Sea Creatures

A TIME-LIFE TELEVISION BOOK

Produced in Association with Vineyard Books, Inc.

Editor: Eleanor Graves
Senior Consultants: Lucille Ogle
Text Editor: Richard Oulahan
Associate Text Editors: Bonnie Johnson, Jack Murphy
Author: Thomas A. Dozier
Assistant Editors: Harold C. Field, Regina Grant Hersey
Literary Research: Ellen Schachter
Text Research: Irene Neves, Elsie Washington
Copy Editors: Robert J. Myer, Peter Ainslie
Picture Editor: Richard O. Pollard
Picture Research: Judith Greene
Permissions: Jo-Anne Cienski
Book Designer and Art Director: Jos. Trautwein
Assistant Art Director: David Russell
Production Coordinator: Jane L. Quinson

WILD, WILD WORLD OF ANIMALS
TELEVISION PROGRAM
Producers: Jonathan Donald and Lothar Wolff
This Time-Life Television Book is published by Time-Life Films, Inc.
Bruce L. Paisner, *President*
J. Nicoll Durrie, *Vice President*

THE AUTHOR

THOMAS A. DOZIER was a foreign correspondent for *Time* and *Life* magazines for 24 years and has also written for *Sports Illustrated, Smithsonian* and *Travel and Camera* magazines. He claims to have "fished or put a foot in" most of the world's major bodies of water, from Lake Titicaca to the South China Sea.

THE CONSULTANTS

DR. BRUCE W. HALSTEAD is a doctor of medicine and biotoxology as well as an internationally recognized authority on poisonous and venomous sea creatures. He has written over 160 articles on the subject and has served as a consultant on marine life to many organizations, including the World Health Organization, the Academy of Sciences of the U.S.S.R., the U. S. Air Force and the state of California.

DR. EUGENIE CLARK, a marine biologist, is presently Professor of Zoology at the University of Maryland. She is an authority on sharks and has done research for many organizations all over the world, including the Atomic Energy Commission, the Office of Naval Research and the National Science Foundation. She is the author of numerous scientific articles, and the book *Lady with a Spear.*

[redacted]

Wild, Wild World of Animals

Dangerous Sea Creatures

Based on the television series
Wild, Wild World of Animals

Published by
TIME-LIFE FILMS

The excerpt from Jaws by Peter Benchley, copyright © 1974 by Peter Benchley, is reprinted by permission of Doubleday & Company, Inc. and André Deutsch, Ltd.

The excerpt from Kon-Tiki by Thor Heyerdahl, copyright 1950 by Thor Heyerdahl, is reprinted by permission of Rand McNally & Co. and George Allen and Unwin Ltd.

The excerpt from The Living Sea by Jacques-Yves Cousteau with James Dugan (Harper hardbound edition), copyright © 1963 by Harper & Row, Publishers, Inc., is reprinted by permission of the publisher.

The excerpts from The Edge of the Sea by Rachel Carson, copyright © 1955 by Rachel L. Carson, are reprinted by permission of Houghton Mifflin Company.

The excerpt from "The Fire in the Galley Stove," copyright 1937 by Captain William Outerson, is reprinted from Davy Jones' Haunted Locker by Robert Arthur by permission of William Outerson, Jr.

The excerpt from the Odyssey by Homer, translated by E. V. Rieu, January 1946, copyright © E. V. Rieu, January 1946, is reprinted by permission of Penguin Books, Ltd.

ISBN 0-913948-04-7

Library of Congress Catalog Card Number: 75-45283

Printed in the United States of America.

Contents

Introduction

by Thomas A. Dozier

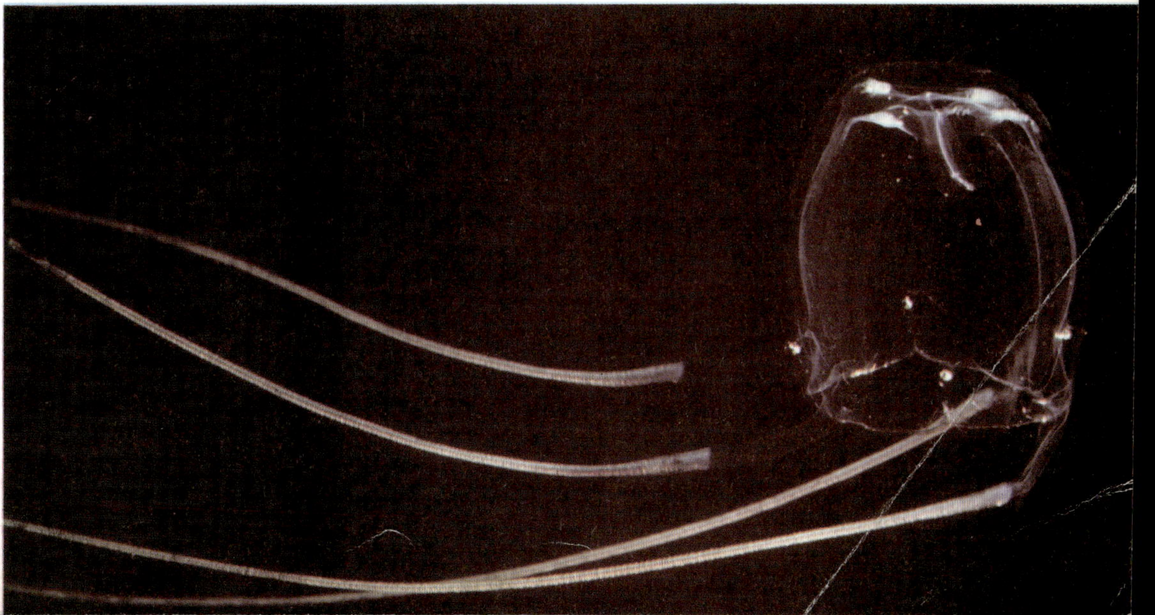

MAN, LIKE ALL LIVING THINGS on this planet, originally came from the sea and is continuously and irresistibly drawn back to the watery element in which his earliest ancestors were spawned. In his imagination and in the poetic articulation of this uniquely human faculty he sees the sea as a place of beginnings and endings, of permanence and change, of tranquillity and tumult—and always of mystery. The mysterious quality of the sea can be a source of joyous meditation, but the joy is inevitably tinged with fear. Herman Melville, who wrote about the sea in soaringly lyrical terms, put it as well as anyone: "There is, one knows not what sweet mystery about the sea, whose gently awful stirrings seem to speak of some hidden soul beneath."

There are so many hidden things beneath that not even the most learned marine scientists claim that all the mysteries of the sea have been solved. Man has sailed his ships on its surface for at least 4,000 years, taken fish for food from its upper levels and bathed on its shores for as long. Ichthyologists as early as Aristotle made detailed studies of the marine life they encountered, not always with scientifically accurate results. "The sea" to the Greeks was only the Mediterranean and its extensions—the Phoenicians had sailed far beyond into both the Atlantic and the Pacific but left few written records—and it was not until the dawn of the Age of Exploration and the daring exploits of brave sailors like Columbus and Magellan that man began to understand the true vastness of the oceans. Even these discoveries dealt only with the surface of the sea. It has been only within the present century, with the development of electronic echo-sounding apparatus, that universal depths could be measured and the true dimensions of the watery world comprehended. Firsthand exploration of these depths has been achieved only in the present century. The most penetrating investigation took place on January 23, 1960, when the bathyscaphe *Trieste* spent 20 minutes at the bottom of the Challenger Deep in the Marianas Trench of the western Pacific—almost seven miles down in the deepest indentation in the planet Earth.

What man has learned about the breadth and depth of the sea makes the name "Earth" seem inappropriate. Something like "Oceanus" would have been more accurate, because almost three fourths of the globe is covered by water. For every square mile of dry land there are two and a half square miles of ocean surface, and the continents are in reality no more than islands jutting out of one single world ocean, dividing it into various entities that we arbitrarily call oceans, seas, gulfs and bays. In terms of cubic measurement, the superior vastness of the marine world over that of the land is even more staggering: There is about 300 times more space in the ocean than on land. The seas contain an estimated 330 million cubic miles of water, irregularly distributed but with an average depth of more than two miles. The earth's highest outcropping, Mount Everest, 29,028 feet, could be sunk in its entirety in the 35,800-foot Marianas Trench, and its peak would still be more than a mile beneath the Pacific's waves. If the earth's surface were smoothed out,

Reef whitetip sharks gather in the Galápagos Islands

This schematic drawing—not to scale—shows many of the dangerous creatures found in different waters around the world and the approximate zones they inhabit. Ninety-eight percent of all marine life, docile and dangerous, lives in the waters above the continental shelf, the platform that surrounds all land masses and that slopes to a depth of 600 feet before the sea floor drops off to abyssal depths. This relatively shallow water (compared with the 36,000-foot depth of the Marianas Trench) is penetrated by sunlight, which aids in the growth of the microscopic plant and animal life, called plankton, that begin the ocean's food chain. Plankton is so abundant in the waters near shore that animals such as hydroids, sea anemones, sea urchins and sea cucumbers anchor themselves to rocks or coral reefs while much of the nourishment they need drifts within their reach. Weever fish, stingrays, skates and octopuses inhabit often cloudy waters close to shore, where they feed on smaller forms of marine life. Swimming freely offshore are porcupine fish, barracudas, sea snakes, manta rays, squids, skates and needlefish. Sharks, like the other creatures shown here, spend most of their lives in the upper 300 feet of the world's waters.

1. *Hydroid*
2. *Jellyfish*
3. *Blenny*
4. *Weever fish*
5. *Sea urchin*
6. *Giant grouper*
7. *Zebra fish*
8. *Scorpion fish*
9. *Stingray*
10. *Porcupine fish*
11. *Sawfish*
12. *Octopus*
13. *Crown-of-thorns sea star*
14. *Puffer fish*
15. *Skate*
16. *Sea anemone*
17. *Sea cucumber*
18. *Portuguese man-of-war*
19. *Needlefish*
20. *Squid*
21. *Sea snakes*
22. *Thresher shark*
23. *Manta ray*
24. *Barracuda*
25. *Tiger shark*
26. *Whale shark*
27. *Hammerhead shark*

leaving no hills, mountains or deeps, the ocean would cover the land to a depth of 8,000 feet.

Fortunately for man and other land-dwelling creatures, this is not likely to happen. If it should, the catastrophe would by no means wipe out life on the planet, because five sixths of all living matter dwells in the upper, sunlit level of the ocean, and scientists have found that life exists, although in scarcer quantities, all the way to the bottom of the deepest trench. There is no way of conceiving of the trillions of individual creatures that dwell in the sea. There are literally hundreds of thousands of different species of marine animals, each one superbly adapted to its environment. The basic goals of all sea creatures, from the tiny diatom to the biggest whale, are to reproduce in whatever manner nature has ordained;

to feed, if necessary, by preying on other living matter; and to move about as the needs of self-defense, feeding and reproduction dictate. (There is a strong suggestion that some higher forms, such as the dolphin and the whale, are capable of more complex drives and emotions, but we are not concerned with marine mammals in this volume.) Although there is no real evidence that sea predators hunt just for the sake of killing, inevitably, in the quest for food and the necessity of defending themselves against man's intrusion, certain sea creatures become a danger.

In general, the aquatic animals that can be harmful to man fall into four categories: the biters, headed by the notorious shark; the stingers, or those that inflict injury by injecting venom into their victims; the poisoners, or those that produce suffering or death when eaten; the shockers, unique in their capability to stun or kill with the electric currents they generate.

The threatening creatures vary enormously, from the four-inch blue-ringed octopus to the 60-foot giant squid, and in between are the manifold varieties of venomous and poisonous marine life of the sea. The measure of danger varies almost as much. Probably one of the most venomous of all is the sea wasp, a small tropical jellyfish that can kill a man within half a minute with the merest touch of its dangling tentacles. Among the poisoners, the comical-looking puffer may be the deadliest. While parts of its flesh are delicious, other parts contain a poison powerful enough to cause the violent death of anyone who eats one. Still other fish—snapper, bonito, mackerel, tuna and skipjack—are eminently edible if caught in certain waters, but they can be highly toxic and cause painful illness, even death, when caught in other areas.

Venomous and poisonous marine life have been known as a danger to man since the beginnings of civilization. Hieroglyphics depicting poisonous puffers have been found on tombs of the Fifth Dynasty of Egypt's Old Kingdom dating from 2700 B.C. The earliest known Chinese pharmacopoeia, which was written between 2833 and 2700 B.C., refers to puffer poisoning. There is a Biblical reference to the danger of poisonous and venomous animals of the sea in the Book of Deuteronomy (14: 9–10). Moses, after laying down the Ten Commandments of God, added this instruction to the Israelites: "Of all that are in the waters you may eat whatever has fins and scales. And whatever does not have fins and scales you shall not eat; it is unclean for you." Like the Hebrew practice of avoiding pork, which can cause the disease trichinosis, this is scientifically sound advice, for it is a fact that many poisonous and venomous sea creatures do indeed appear to be scaleless or finless. Notable examples are the puffer among the poisoners and almost all the venomous sea animals: the stingray, toadfish, stonefish, moray eel, blue-ringed octopus, Portuguese man-of-war, sea wasp—the list of those without scales and with envenomating potential seems endless.

In fact, the list of dangerous sea creatures is so long and so varied, and the animals are found in such familiar and beautiful surroundings, that a careful and contemplative researcher into such things might be tempted to make a firm resolution never to enter the sea again or to eat anything taken from it. Before succumbing to such fear, some basic truths should be clearly stated and accepted. One is that only the most elementary precautions are necessary to avoid eating poisonous marine flesh. The others are overwhelmingly reassuring to the bather and diver: With the exception of a few species of sharks, no creature in the sea will attack man without provocation, and none puts human flesh high on its menu of favorite foods.

Compared to man, the shark is a piker as a killer. The number of homicides in the world in any one year exceeds all fatal shark attacks in all the centuries since record-keeping began. And if the millions killed in man's wars over the ages, the multitude of bodies left mangled on highways and the uncountable hordes of nonhuman animals wantonly slaughtered are all added to the list of man-attack victims, the shark dwindles into insignificance.

Just as he is the deadliest animal on land, man is the most dangerous creature in, on and around the sea. He has abused many species to the point of extinction, slaughtering the great whales by the hundreds of thousands for their oil and whalebone or at times because some species—such as the huge sperm whale—were also considered to be consuming too much fish. Man himself has constantly mechanized and improved his own fish-catching capacity to the point that many segments of the world ocean, such as the Mediterranean, are all but fished out. In recent years man has recognized that such wholesale slaughter cannot continue without irreversibly damaging the natural balance of life on the planet, and international conventions have halted some of the indiscriminate killing. But this is only a beginning—an important one because it shows that *Homo sapiens* has finally realized that he cannot, without risk to himself, impose his unfettered and aggressive will on the other animals with whom he shares the common resources of the sea. But now a subtler and more dangerous menace is growing: pollution.

For thousands of years man in his ever-multiplying numbers has used the sea as his ultimate cesspool and garbage dump, emptying thousands of tons of his effluents directly into it or into streams, lakes and rivers that carry it eventually to the sea. In more recent years he has added to the wastes the oil spillage from tankers and underwater wells. As a result, he has already upset the essential food chain that, beginning with the tiny planktonic creatures, not only maintains the infinitely varied life of the sea but also, through the delicate symbiotic relationship of all living things, provides man with the basic necessities of life as we know it: breathable air, edible food, potable water and tolerable climate. The sea is not only the cradle and generator of these essentials; it is also the great moderator of the fundamental conditions that make life possible on earth. If man should destroy totally the fauna of the sea, which he is well on his way to doing, he would destroy all life, including his own. Thus the most dangerous sea predator is neither shark, cephalopod or some sinister sea monster. It is man himself.

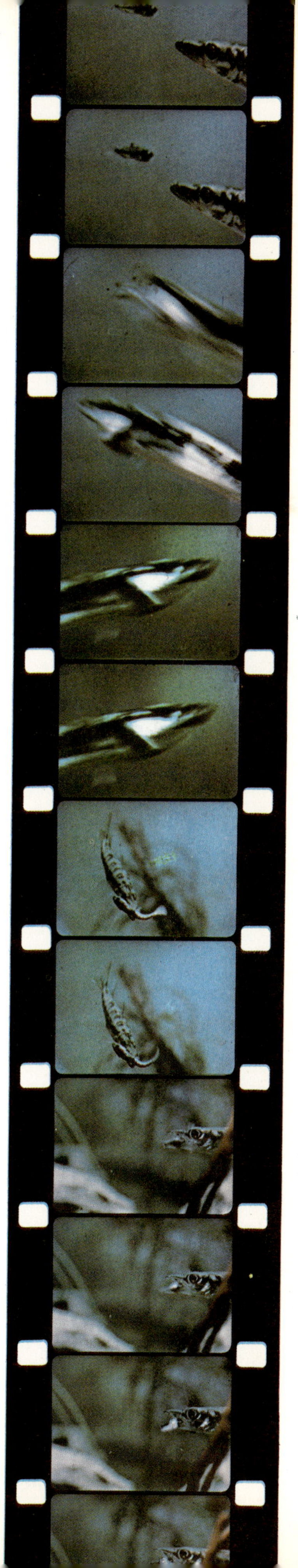

Sharks

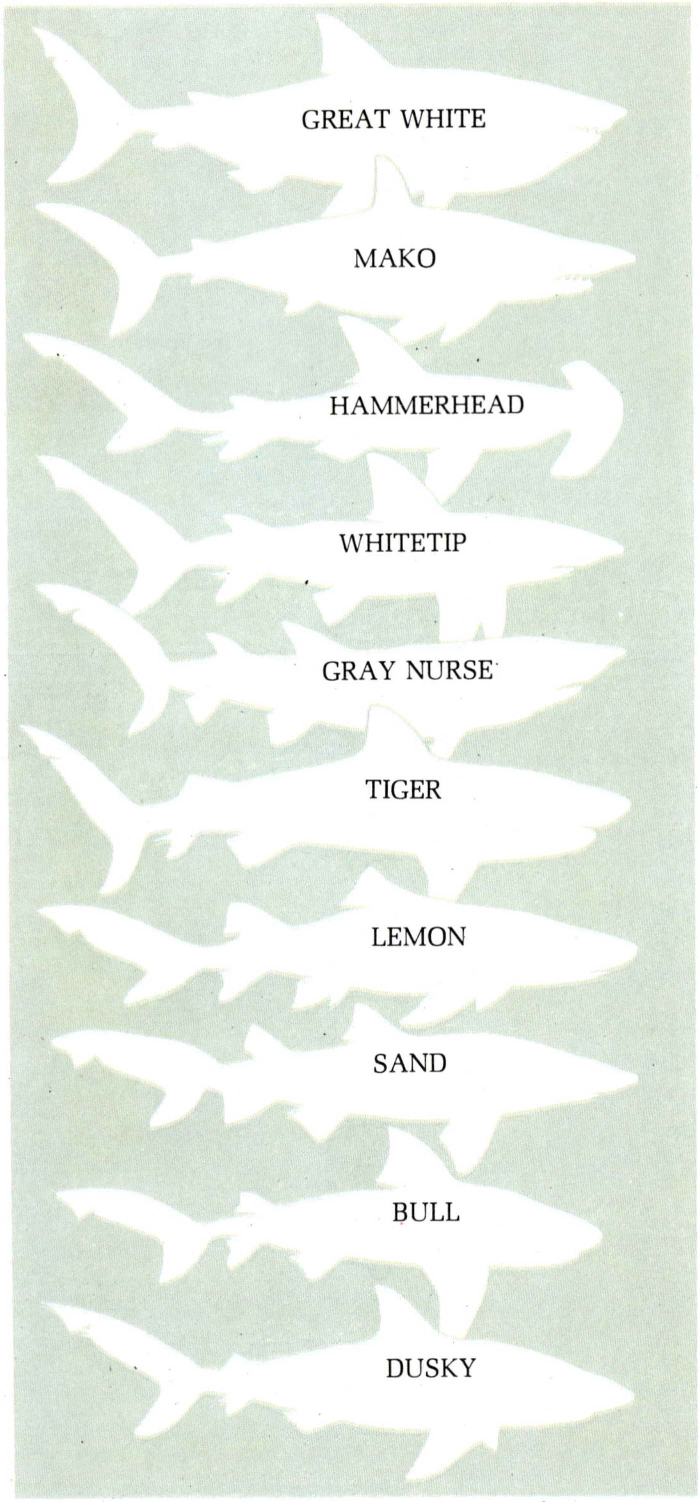

Of all the creatures that roam the seas, the most hated and feared is the shark. A prehistoric predator that has fired man's fantasies for thousands of years, the shark was studied by scholars as early as Aristotle (384–322 B.C.), who made precise notes on its anatomy and behavior. In the first century A.D., Pliny the Elder wrote of the "cruel combat that sponge fishermen must maintain against the dogfish [shark]," warning that the danger of being attacked by a shark increased as a diver neared the water's surface, an observation shared by many contemporary diving experts. Although only 39 of the 250 extant species of sharks have been involved in attacks on humans, they are enough to give the whole family a bad name. The natural fear sharks inspire was exploited on an unprecedented scale in *Jaws*, the best-selling novel and film of 1974–75.

The best available evidence suggests that the shark evolved roughly into its present form 100 million years ago. Watching a modern shark—preferably through the protective glass walls of an aquarium—is like looking down the corridor of evolution into the far-distant past. As that distinguished undersea mariner Captain Jacques-Yves Cousteau puts it: "Across the gulf of ages . . . the relentless, indestructible shark has come without need of evolution, the oldest killer, armed for the fray of existence in the beginning."

Designed for the fray so many millions of years ago, the shark is superbly suited to the purpose of attacking and

The illustration at left is of ten species of sharks known to have attacked humans. These are listed on the United States Navy's "Shark Danger" ratings list. The silhouettes accurately portray the differences in form among these species but are not drawn to scale. The "Shark Danger" list is only one result of the efforts made by the Navy, in cooperation with the Smithsonian Institution, to find out more about shark attacks and the factors that lead to predacious activity in the hope of diminishing future catastrophes. Information on 1,652 cases of shark attacks on humans—known collectively as the International Shark Attack File—was analyzed. Of these, 1,165 cases were deemed valid enough to code and computerize and were statistically broken down into categories such as wound characteristics, where attacks took place and diversionary actions. The file on the number of attacks inflicted by each species revealed the great white shark as the most pernicious of all, with 32 attacks attributed to it. The tiger shark was a close second, with 27 strikes against it, while a lesser demon, the dusky shark, was implicated in only two attacks.

eating. In most species the mouth is positioned well back in the head, beneath the snout, an arrangement that has led to the belief that sharks must turn on their backs or sides to bite. This is not true. Sharks frequently attack from below, angling the snout upward and over the target, which then can be ravaged by the animal's fearsome teeth. It is this unusual dental equipment that sets the shark apart from most other carnivores of land and sea. Unlike the teeth of vertebrates such as humans, which are anchored to the jaws by roots, shark dentures are imbedded in the gums to form four to six rows—as many as 20 in some species—of razor-sharp teeth. The teeth move steadily forward as they increase in size, falling out when they are used and being replaced by those moving up from behind. It has been estimated that a single tiger shark may produce, use and shed as many as 24,000 teeth in a 10-year period. A shark thus might be described as one massive conglomerate of teeth—which is appropriate enough for a creature whose notoriety is based on its bite.

That bite has a telltale crescent shape; it is jagged and, depending on the size and ferocity of the shark, often very deep. Besides people, the shark may attack and devour just about anything that comes within its range: dolphins, sea turtles, sea lions, birds, fish, land animals that have fallen into or taken to the water. The shark itself has as few natural enemies as it has natural friends. The killer whale and the swordfish will sometimes give pursuit to a shark, but under normal circumstances it is preyed upon only by its own kind, and the usual fate of an aging or infirm shark is to be eaten by other sharks.

With its insatiable appetite, the killer shark has no hesitation about swallowing dead or inanimate objects. One shark killed off an Australian dock had in its stomach half a ham, several legs of mutton, the head and forelegs of a bulldog with a rope around its neck, a quantity of horseflesh and a ship's scraper. Another, taken in the Adriatic Sea, contained three overcoats (but not their wearers), a raincoat and an automobile license plate. To accommodate such weird meals, the shark is equipped with a distensible stomach that can expand to several times its normal size. What is more remarkable is that a shark can apparently store food or foreign objects for weeks at a time without digesting them. Some ichthyologists have

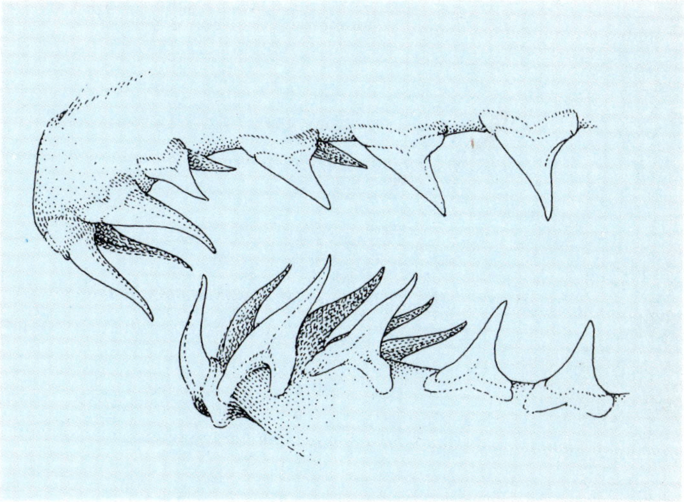

The jagged upper and lower front teeth of the mako shark

suggested that the Biblical Jonah was swallowed and later regurgitated not by a whale but by a large shark.

Aside from these gastrointestinal eccentricities, the characteristics that distinguish the shark from other fish are a skeleton of gristle or cartilage instead of bone, the lack of an air bladder and a highly developed reproductive system. Having a cartilaginous rather than a bony skeleton has been no handicap for the shark, and certainly the shark has been successful for several hundred million years with its gristly structure. But the absence of an air bladder, a flotation device that permits other fish to stay at a given depth without effort, means that many sharks must keep moving or sink (although one species, the sand tiger shark, can hold enough air in its stomach to make it buoyant for hours at a time). For that reason it is generally assumed that most sharks never sleep—although some marine biologists have found them "dozing" in underwater caves.

The activity in which the shark holds an advantage over its bony cousins is sex. Whereas most fish discharge eggs and semen into the water and leave them to unite and develop haphazardly at sea, male and female sharks copulate. The male has auxiliary genital organs called "claspers," which it uses to penetrate the female orifice (covered with a hymenlike membrane in maiden sharks, a fact discovered by no less reputable an investigator than Aristotle) for introduction of the seminal fluid, a process that may take over 20 minutes. Once fertilized, the female gestates her young in the manner and in the number—from one to over 100 per litter—appropriate to her species. Some lay unhatched eggs; others produce live young nurtured in the womb in the fashion of mammals, while still others form eggs that are hatched within the mother, who then brings forth live sharklets, or pups, as they are properly known. Nearly all newborn sharks are fully equipped with teeth and are prepared immediately to begin their own defense and quest for food.

Sharks have a very finely tuned sensory system for finding the food with which to satisfy their hunger. Vibrations from an animal in the water as far as 600 feet away are picked up by nerve endings that extend along the animal's body from snout to tail. This is known as the "lateral line," and the vibrations may register on the shark's brain as sound. Once the sensation registers, the shark can bring into play one of the keenest senses of smell in the animal kingdom: It can sniff an ounce of fish blood in a million ounces of water. Notoriously nearsighted, sharks are believed to rely on their eyes only when they come quite close to their prey. They begin circling at about 10 feet and, depending on the species and momentary inclinations, may or may not close in for an attack.

There are some 250 species of sharks, ranging in size from six inches to 45 or possibly even 60 feet. Fortunately the two largest—the basking shark of temperate waters and the whale shark of the tropics—are gentle plankton-eaters. But the whale shark, pushing its huge mouth through the water to filter 400,000 gallons an hour for plankton, takes in all sorts of objects, from discarded crates and trunks to other large fish that follow the plankton into the huge maw.

Of the other species and subspecies, no one is quite certain just how many should be considered dangerous to man. In the International Shark Attack File maintained by the U.S. Navy and the Smithsonian Institution in Washington, D.C., no fewer than 39 different species are listed as having been implicated in attacks on humans. Those that are most frequently placed in the man-eating category are the formidable great white; the tiger; the mako and its relatives; the deadly gray nurse of Australian and South African waters; the hammerhead; the sand shark; and a collection of villains, lumped under the appropriate family name of requiem sharks, that includes the brown, the dusky, the great blue, the blacktip, the whitetip and the lemon. There is one recognized freshwater marauder, the bull shark, also called the Lake Nicaragua shark, which inhabits a 100-mile-long lake of the same name in Central America. It is also known as the Ganges shark, which has developed a taste for the cadavers of pious Indians ceremoniously committed to that sacred river and its tributary, the Hooghly. This species seems to make little distinction between the quick and the dead and goes after bathers as well as corpses.

Among all the man-killers of river, lake and sea, the dread great white shark fully deserves the title of Most Deadly. It is the biggest of the man-eaters, the largest specimen ever caught measuring 21 feet and weighing more than three tons. It is also the most powerful and the most voracious, standing convicted in the Navy–Smithsonian Shark Attack File of the greatest number of assaults on human beings of all sharks. The great white attacks in warm waters and cool, in the shallows and in the depths, nearly always without warning and frequently with fatal results due to the power of its charge and the size of its teeth and mouth. A report from Australia has it that one great white was taken with the remains of a whole horse in its belly. In 1916 a shark fatally attacked four bathers and mutilated a fifth in a few days along a stretch of the New Jersey coast, setting off the greatest shark hunt in the nation's history. Although the fish was never caught, based on the available evidence, most experts concluded that the culprit was a great white.

The great white is the archetype of the carnivorous shark. During World War II literally thousands of victims of ship disasters were consumed by sharks as they struggled in the water, but by far the greatest number of authenticated attacks have occurred with the victim standing waist deep in or swimming on the surface of the sea within 10 to 50 yards of shore.

On the subject of shark attack, probably the all-time understatement is that made by H. David Baldridge in the preface to his excellent book summarizing the results of the U.S. Navy–Smithsonian study of 1,600 man-shark confrontations from the 16th century to the present. "Shark attack is unique among human experiences," wrote Baldridge. "What could possibly equal being eaten alive by a monster fish?"

Built for Battle

In the fish-eat-fish world of the sea, the shark is king of all predators. It kills to eat, to assert its dominance over another being or to eliminate what it perceives as a threat to itself. Of all the sharks, the great white, shown on these pages, is the most fearsome, a fish superbly adapted for hunting in its watery domain. Its sensitive olfactory system gives the shark the ability to smell prey over a quarter of a mile away. A hunting shark also depends on its eyesight, especially, it is believed, when the shark gets within about 100 feet of its prey. The shark's "hearing" apparatus consists of a series of liquid-filled canals connected to the outer skin by pores that run the entire length of the shark's body and fan out across its face. As vibrations reach the pores, the liquid in the canals is stimulated and sends impulses to the fish's brain. Erratic vibrations, like those made by a wounded fish or a drowning person, most easily attract the shark's attention, and from their intensity the shark seems able to determine their source and distance.

The white shark's streamlined shape allows it to move effortlessly and speedily through the water. It has a denticle-covered, sandpaper skin and sharp fins, notably the sinister dorsal fin that sticks out of the water (left), which are capable of inflicting serious injury. The white shark (below) chews on the leg of a horse, a free meal thrown to it by a team of research scientists.

JAWS

by Peter Benchley

The year 1974–75 proved to be the year of the shark—not on the Chinese calendar but in the minds of the thousands who read Peter Benchley's novel Jaws *and saw the motion picture based on the book. Mr. Benchley, third in the line of authors in the Benchley family, creates a picture so vivid, a situation so realistic that many who read or saw* Jaws *became acutely aware of the terrors that lurk beneath the surface of the water. In the following excerpt the great white shark, one of the most savage of the earth's creatures, claims its first victim off the shore of Amity, the fictional resort community that serves as the setting for the novel.*

The great fish moved silently through the night water, propelled by short sweeps of its crescent tail. The mouth was open just enough to permit a rush of water over the gills. There was little other motion: an occasional correction of the apparently aimless course by the slight raising or lowering of a pectoral fin—as a bird changes direction by dipping one wing and lifting the other. The eyes were sightless in the black, and the other senses transmitted nothing extraordinary to the small, primitive brain. The fish might have been asleep, save for the movement dictated by countless millions of years of instinctive continuity: lacking the flotation bladder common to other fish and the fluttering flaps to push oxygen-bearing water through its gills, it survived only by moving. Once stopped, it would sink to the bottom and die of anoxia.

The land seemed almost as dark as the water, for there was no moon. All that separated sea from shore was a long, straight stretch of beach—so white that it shone. From a house behind the grass-splotched dunes, lights cast yellow glimmers on the sand.

The front door to the house opened, and a man and a woman stepped out onto the wooden porch. They stood for a moment staring at the sea, embraced quickly, and scampered down the few steps onto the sand. The man was drunk, and he stumbled on the bottom step. The woman laughed and took his hand, and together they ran to the beach. . . .

The woman walked to where the gentle surf washed over her ankles. The water was colder than the night air, for it was only mid-June. The woman called back, "You're sure you don't want to come?" But there was no answer. . . .

She backed up a few steps, then ran at the water. At first her strides were long and graceful, but then a small wave crashed into her knees. She faltered, regained her footing, and flung herself over the next waist-high wave. The water was only up to her hips, so she stood, pushed the hair out of her eyes, and continued walking until the water covered her shoulders. There she began to swim—with the jerky, head-above-water stroke of the untutored.

A hundred yards offshore, the fish sensed a change in the sea's rhythm. It did not see the woman, nor yet did it smell her. Running within the length of its body were a series of thin canals, filled with mucus and dotted with nerve endings, and these nerves detected vibrations and signaled the brain. The fish turned toward shore.

The woman continued to swim away from the beach, stopping now and then to check her position by the lights shining from the house. The tide was slack, so she had not moved up or down the beach. But she was tiring, so she rested for a moment, treading water, and then started for shore.

The vibrations were stronger now, and the fish recog-

nized prey. The sweeps of its tail quickened, thrusting the giant body forward with a speed that agitated the tiny phosphorescent animals in the water and caused them to glow, casting a mantle of sparks over the fish.

The fish closed on the woman and hurtled past, a dozen feet to the side and six feet below the surface. The woman felt only a wave of pressure that seemed to lift her up in the water and ease her down again. She stopped swimming and held her breath. Feeling nothing further, she resumed her lurching stroke.

The fish smelled her now, and the vibrations—erratic and sharp—signaled distress. The fish began to circle close to the surface. Its dorsal fin broke water, and its tail, thrashing back and forth, cut the glassy surface with a hiss. A series of tremors shook its body.

For the first time, the woman felt fear, though she did not know why. Adrenaline shot through her trunk and her limbs, generating a tingling heat and urging her to swim faster. She guessed that she was fifty yards from shore. She could see the line of white foam where the waves broke on the beach. She saw the lights in the house, and for a comforting moment she thought she saw someone pass by one of the windows.

The fish was about forty feet from the woman, off to the side, when it turned suddenly to the left, dropped entirely below the surface, and, with two quick thrusts of its tail, was upon her.

At first, the woman thought she had snagged her leg on a rock or a piece of floating wood. There was no initial pain, only one violent tug on her right leg. She reached down to touch her foot, treading water with her left leg to keep her head up, feeling in the blackness with her left hand. She could not find her foot. She reached higher on her leg, and then she was overcome by a rush of nausea and dizziness. Her groping fingers had found a nub of bone and tattered flesh. She knew that the warm, pulsing flow over her fingers in the chill water was her own blood.

Pain and panic struck together. The woman threw her head back and screamed a guttural cry of terror.

The fish had moved away. It swallowed the woman's limb without chewing. Bones and meat passed down the massive gullet in a single spasm. Now the fish turned again, homing on the stream of blood flushing from the woman's femoral artery, a beacon as clear and true as a lighthouse on a cloudless night. This time the fish attacked from below. It hurtled up under the woman, jaws agape. The great conical head struck her like a locomotive, knocking her up out of the water. The jaws snapped shut around her torso, crushing bones and flesh and organs into a jelly. The fish, with the woman's body in its mouth, smashed down on the water with a thunderous splash, spewing foam and blood and phosphorescence in a gaudy shower.

Below the surface, the fish shook its head from side to side, its serrated triangular teeth sawing through what little sinew still resisted. The corpse fell apart. The fish swallowed, then turned to continue feeding. Its brain still registered the signals of nearby prey. The water was laced with blood and shreds of flesh, and the fish could not sort signal from substance. It cut back and forth through the dissipating cloud of blood, opening and closing its mouth, seining for a random morsel. But by now, most of the pieces of the corpse had dispersed. A few sank slowly, coming to rest on the sandy bottom, where they moved lazily in the current. A few drifted away just below the surface, floating in the surge that ended in the surf.

A deadly great white shark (below) approaches its prey with its gaping jaws exposing awesome two-inch teeth. In seizing its victim the shark moves its upper jaw forward, slicing off enormous chunks of flesh. If its prey is not very large, the shark will gulp it down whole.

The Jaws of Death

Shark teeth are arranged in rows, with some fish having as few as five and others as many as 20 formidable tiers. When a fish is not biting, only the first row is fully erect. The remaining teeth, which are in various stages of formation, lie flat beneath a membrane but can be raised during an attack. As if on a conveyor belt, worn-out or dislodged teeth are replaced within 24 hours by the next tooth in line. New teeth are always larger than their predecessors, keeping up with the growth of the shark's body. It is believed that sharks were the first animals to develop teeth. The dentition of the different species of sharks shows tremendous diversity. There are (below, from the top) the saw-edged teeth of the tiger shark, the jagged teeth of the thresher, the sand shark's stiletto-like teeth and the angled, razor-sharp fangs of the hammerhead. The unmistakable serrated triangles of the great white are completely unlike the broad, blunt teeth of certain species of dogfish, one of the smallest of the sharks.

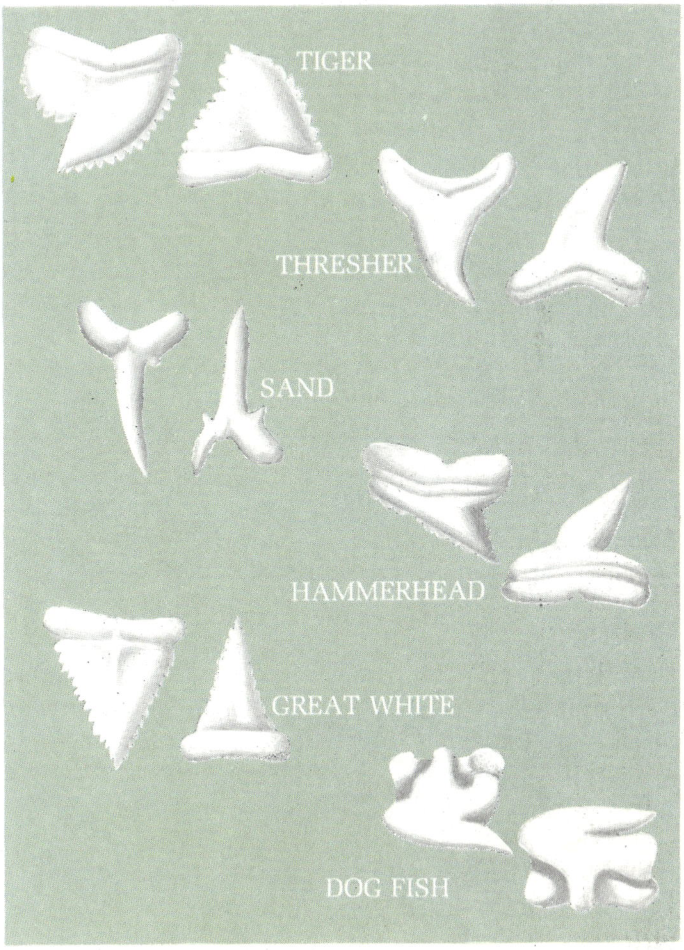

The Great White's Killer Cousins

The great whites, the makos and the porbeagle sharks (seen in the drawing below) are commonly called mackerel sharks because of their distinctive mackerel- or half-moon-shaped tails. Although the porbeagle has been less publicized than its notorious cousin, the great white, it is potentially as dangerous. Porbeagles grow to a length of up to about 13 feet and are found in the open waters of the North Atlantic Ocean as well as the Mediterranean, Baltic and North seas. They are fast swimmers that are often seen following large schools of mackerels, herrings and sardines that, along with bottom-dwelling fish and cephalopods, make up most of their diet.

Until 1961, when its first attack on a bather was reported in the United States, the sand tiger shark (left) was considered harmless. Among the most numerous sharks, the sand shark is found in both sides of the Atlantic Ocean, from the hump of western Africa and the Canary and Cape Verde islands in the east to the Gulf of Maine, Florida and Brazil in the west. This shark is distinguished by its ability to swallow air and hold it in its stomach, creating a kind of air bladder, an organ sharks normally lack, which enables it to float.

The tiger shark, a distinct species from the sand tiger, is easy to recognize by the striped markings that are quite prominent in the young and become paler as the fish ages. Growing to a length of about 20 feet, the shark (right) usually moves lethargically, but in pursuit of prey it becomes a determined and swift swimmer. The tiger shark is common to tropical waters and is especially feared in the coastal areas of the West Indies, Australia and India, where it habitually roams shallow waters for food. It has been known to eat anything from stingrays to chicken coops. Like all requiem sharks, the tiger shark's mouth has joints at either end and in the center of its upper and lower jaws, which permit the mouth to distend to accommodate objects almost as large as itself.

The nurse shark (left) is a large (up to 10 feet long), slow-moving creature with a short, rounded snout. Its small teeth and powerful jaws give it a dentition better suited to crushing than biting. In many attacks on humans the nurse shark has demonstrated this by clamping its jaws so tightly onto its victim that only by killing the fish could it be dislodged.

The oceanic whitetip shark (above) is an inhabitant of the warm waters of the Atlantic, the Gulf of Mexico, the Caribbean and the Pacific. Like all sharks, it is often escorted by small, striped pilot fish and by remoras. These fish remove the annoying parasites that plague sharks and feed on the sharks' scraps. The gray reef shark (below) is found in the Indian and Pacific oceans, where it has been implicated in a number of attacks on humans. A treacherous inhabitant of Australia's coastal waters is the wobbegong (opposite). Its varied markings help conceal it as it waits for prey, which is usually fish, not man, although the wobbegong has been identified in some attacks on bathers.

Surrounded by young barjacks, a reef shark (below) lies docilely on the floor of an underwater cave off the coast of Mexico. For as yet unexplained reasons, the natural conditions in this grotto have a tranquilizing effect on even usually savage sharks, such as the reef shark, a member of the requiem shark family that includes some of the world's most notorious man-eaters.

Alias the Bull Shark

After a day spent prowling for food, a reef shark (opposite) lies in repose, its staring eye the only clue that, no matter how immobile it may appear, the shark is not truly asleep. This is a rare position for most sharks, which must swim constantly to keep water flowing over their gills. The unblinking eye below is that of a bull shark. This fish inhabits numerous bodies of fresh and salt water around the world, and in almost every geographic area it bears a different name. Its reputation as a killer is well deserved, especially the freshwater varieties, which include the Lake Nicaragua and Ganges sharks of Central America and India, respectively, and the Zambezi shark of South Africa, seen in the pictures at right. The full-grown, captive Zambezi shark (top picture) selects its prey, a young gray shark (second picture). After getting a bite on the smaller shark's tail (third picture), the Zambezi shark then shifts its grip (bottom picture) in preparation for devouring its quarry. The somewhat less vicious saltwater versions of the bull shark (also called the cub shark and, in Australia, the whaler) swim slowly in shallow coastal waters and scavenge for most of their food. When food is scarce, however, the 10-foot 400-pounders will unhesitatingly become predators. Like all sharks, however, the bull shark will not eat putrefied flesh.

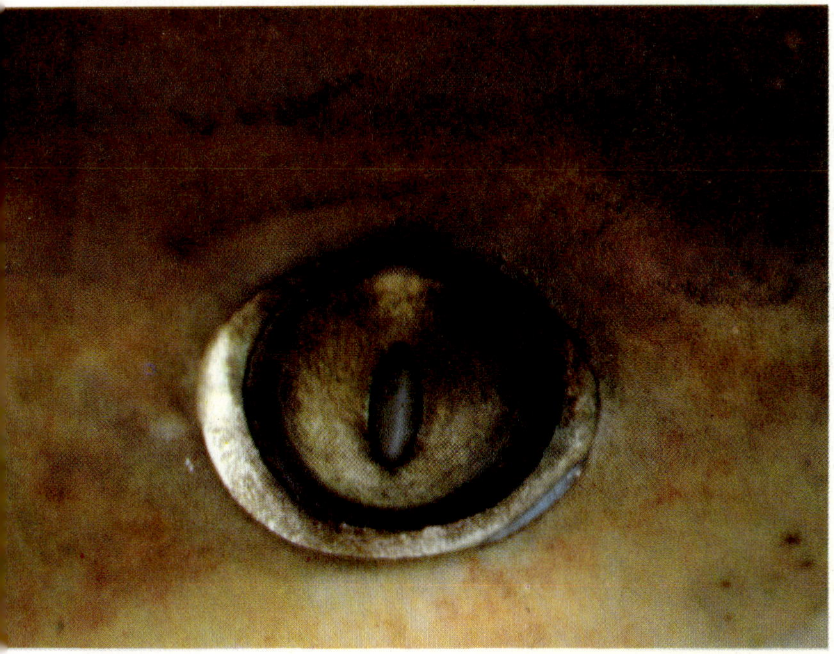

KON-TIKI *by Thor Heyerdahl*

In order to prove his theory that Polynesia might have been settled by white men from Peru rather than by Orientals, as most scholars believed, Norwegian zoologist Thor Heyerdahl set sail from Peru on the balsa-wood raft Kon-Tiki *with five companions. His record of the 4,300-mile, 101-day journey to Polynesia was later published as a book, aptly titled* Kon-Tiki. *Below, Heyerdahl describes his dramatic encounter with the whale shark, the world's biggest fish.*

We gradually grew accustomed to having these subterranean or submarine creatures under the floor, but nevertheless we were just as surprised every time a new species appeared. About two o'clock on a cloudy night, when the man at the helm had difficulty in distinguishing black water from black sky, he caught sight of a faint illumination down in the water which slowly took the shape of a large animal. It was impossible to say whether it was plankton shining on its body, or whether the animal itself had a phosphorescent surface, but the glimmer down in the black water gave the ghostly creature obscure, wavering outlines. Sometimes it was roundish, sometimes oval, or triangular, and suddenly it split into two parts which swam to and fro under the raft independently of each other. Finally there were three of these large shining phantoms wandering round in slow circles under us.

They were real monsters, for the visible parts alone were some five fathoms long, and we all quickly collected on deck and followed the ghost dance. It went on for hour after hour, following the course of the raft. Mysterious and noiseless, our shining companions kept a good way beneath the surface, mostly on the starboard side where the light was, but often they were right under the raft or appeared on the port side. The glimmer of light on their backs revealed that the beasts were bigger than elephants but they were not whales, for they never came up to breathe. Were they giant ray fish which changed shape when they turned over on their sides? They took no notice at all if we held the light right down on the surface to lure them up, so that we might see what kind of creatures they were. And, like all proper goblins and ghosts, they had sunk into the depths when the dawn began to break.

We never got a proper explanation of this nocturnal visit from the three shining monsters, unless the solution was afforded by another visit we received a day and a half later in the full midday sunshine. It was May 24, and we were lying drifting on a leisurely swell in exactly 95° west by 7° south. It was about noon, and we had thrown overboard the guts of two big dolphins we had caught earlier in the morning. I was having a refreshing plunge overboard at the bow, lying in the water but keeping a

good lookout and hanging on to a rope end, when I caught sight of a thick brown fish, six feet long, which came swimming inquisitively toward me through the crystal-clear sea water. I hopped quickly up on the edge of the raft and sat in the hot sun looking at the fish as it passed quietly, when I heard a wild war whoop from Knut, who was sitting aft behind the bamboo cabin. He bellowed "Shark!" till his voice cracked in a falsetto, and, as we had sharks swimming alongside the raft almost daily without creating such excitement, we all realized that this must be something extra-special and flocked astern to Knut's assistance.

Knut had been squatting there, washing his pants in the swell, and when he looked up for a moment he was staring straight into the biggest and ugliest face any of us had ever seen in the whole of our lives. It was the head of a veritable sea monster, so huge and so hideous that, if the Old Man of the Sea himself had come up, he could not have made such an impression on us. The head was broad and flat like a frog's, with two small eyes right at the sides, and a toadlike jaw which was four or five feet wide and had long fringes drooping from the corners of the mouth. Behind the head was an enormous body ending in a long thin tail with a pointed tail fin which stood straight up and showed that this sea monster was not any kind of whale. The body looked brownish under the water, but both head and body were thickly covered with small white spots.

The monster came quietly, lazily swimming after us from astern. It grinned like a bulldog and lashed gently with its tail. The large round dorsal fin projected clear of the water and sometimes the tail fin as well, and, when the creature was in the trough of the swell, the water flowed about the broad back as though washing round a submerged reef. In front of the broad jaws swam a whole crowd of zebra-striped pilot fish in fan formation, and large remora fish and other parasites sat firmly attached to the huge body and traveled with it through the water, so that the whole thing looked like a curious zoological collection crowded round something that resembled a floating deep-water reef.

A twenty-five-pound dolphin, attached to six of our largest fishhooks, was hanging behind the raft as bait for sharks, and a swarm of the pilot fish shot straight off, nosed the dolphin without touching it, and then hurried back to their lord and master, the sea king. Like a mechanical monster it set its machinery going and came gliding at leisure toward the dolphin which lay, a beggarly trifle, before its jaws. We tried to pull the dolphin in, and the sea monster followed slowly, right up to the side of the raft. It did not open its mouth but just let the dolphin bump against it, as if to throw open the whole door for such an insignificant scrap was not worth while. When the giant came close up to the raft, it rubbed its back against the heavy steering oar, which was just lifted up out of the water, and now we had ample opportunity of studying the monster at the closest quarters—at such close quarters that I thought we had all gone mad, for we roared stupidly with laughter and shouted overexcitedly at the completely fantastic sight we saw. Walt Disney himself, with all his powers of imagination, could not have created a more hair-raising sea monster than that which thus suddenly lay with its terrific jaws along the raft's side.

The monster was a whale shark, the largest shark and the largest fish known in the world today. It is exceedingly rare, but scattered specimens are observed here and there in the tropical oceans. The whale shark has an average length of fifty feet, and according to zoologists it weighs fifteen tons. It is said that large specimens can attain a length of sixty feet; one harpooned baby had a liver weighing six hundred pounds and a collection of three thousand teeth in each of its broad jaws.

Our monster was so large that, when it began to swim in

circles round us and under the raft, its head was visible on one side while the whole of its tail stuck out on the other. And so incredibly grotesque, inert, and stupid did it appear when seen fullface that we could not help shouting with laughter, although we realized that it had strength enough in its tail to smash both balsa logs and ropes to pieces if it attacked us. Again and again it described narrower and narrower circles just under the raft, while all we could do was to wait and see what might happen. When it appeared on the other side, it glided amiably under the steering oar and lifted it up in the air, while the oar blade slid along the creature's back.

We stood round the raft with hand harpoons ready for action, but they seemed to us like toothpicks in relation to the mammoth beast we had to deal with. There was no indication that the whale shark ever thought of leaving us again; it circled round us and followed like a faithful dog, close up to the raft. None of us had ever experienced or thought we should experience anything like it; the whole adventure, with the sea monster swimming behind and under the raft, seemed to us so completely unnatural that we could not really take it seriously.

In reality the whale shark went on encircling us for barely an hour, but to us the visit seemed to last a whole day. At last it became too exciting for Erik, who was standing at a corner of the raft with an eight-foot hand harpoon, and, encouraged by ill-considered shouts, he raised the harpoon above his head. As the whale shark came gliding slowly toward him and its broad head moved right under the corner of the raft, Erik thrust the harpoon with all his giant strength down between his legs and deep into the whale shark's gristly head. It was a second or two before the giant understood properly what was happening. Then in a flash the placid half-wit was transformed into a mountain of steel muscles.

We heard a swishing noise as the harpoon line rushed over the edge of the raft and saw a cascade of water as the giant stood on its head and plunged down into the depths. The three men who were standing nearest were flung about the place, head over heels, and two of them were flayed and burned by the line as it rushed through the air. The thick line, strong enough to hold a boat, was caught up on the side of the raft but snapped at once like a piece of twine, and a few seconds later a broken-off harpoon shaft came up to the surface two hundred yards away. A shoal of frightened pilot fish shot off through the water in a desperate attempt to keep up with their old lord and master. We waited a long time for the monster to come racing back like an infuriated submarine, but we never saw anything more of him.

A Hammerhead and an Angel

Because they belong to the same class of cartilaginous fish—Chondrichthyes—there are many sharks, such as the angel shark (above), whose anatomy is remarkably similar to that of rays. The location of the gill slits is the principal feature that distinguishes such sharks from rays. The sharks' gill slits are on the sides in front of their pectoral fins, while the rays' are on the ventral, or lower, surface under the pectoral fins. The hammerhead shark (opposite), on the other hand, with its flattened and elongated head, resembles no other fish in the sea. An eye and a nostril are located at each end of the hammer-shaped head. It is believed that this distinctive form acts as a balancing and steering aid for the hammerhead as well as helping it hunt more effectively by giving it a wider path of water to sample. The largest of the nearly dozen species of hammerheads grows to 18 feet and weighs over 1,000 pounds.

The eggs of oviparous sharks, like the one at left, show great variety in their protective casings. They vary in shape from oval to rectangular and in color from amber to black, yellow or brown. The cases themselves may be striated or smooth. Besides the embryo and its food or yolk sac, the case also contains a fluid similar to the albumen in a chicken's egg. The four outer corners of the case form long threads that attach themselves to rocks or other stationary objects on the sea floor. These anchor the egg during its six- to ten-month development.

Perpetuating the Species

All sharks, from the behemoth 45-foot whale shark to the diminutive six-inch *Squaliolus laticaudus* (so rare it hasn't been given a common name), are fertilized internally, but subsequent development of the young varies with the different species. Some sharks, such as the whale and the cat sharks, are oviparous and lay eggs that are enclosed in a protective horny casing. Others, such as the hammerhead and the whitetip sharks, are viviparous, or live-bearing, producing eggs that develop in a womblike cavity within the female's two oviducts and giving birth to pups. The young are nourished within the womb first by the yolk sac and then by the mother through a special placental connection. A third group, including the thresher and mako sharks, are ovoviviparous. They form eggs that hatch within the mother and then, after feeding from their yolk sacs and maturing further, they are born again into the outside world. Reproduction in the sand tiger, an ovoviviparous shark, is unique in that one embryo in each oviduct feeds on eggs that the female continues to shed through her pregnancy. This prebirth cannibalism results in a litter of only two young, which is in contrast to the 80 or more offspring delivered of egg-laying, oviparous, sharks.

The drawing at right illustrates copulation between cat sharks, during which the male coils himself around the female. Other species mate lying side to side. Although some mysteries remain regarding shark reproduction, certain basic facts are known. Male sharks are equipped with two cartilaginous appendages called claspers, located between the pelvic fins. Fertilization takes place when the male injects sperm into the female's oviducts by means of its claspers. When the young of any shark species are born (like the tiger sharks below) they are miniature duplicates of their parents.

Rays, Skates and Sawfish

Besides the shark, some other noteworthy members of the class of cartilaginous fish called Chondrichthyes include the ray, the skate and the sawfish. Of these, the ray is the most dangerous, for, although none of its 100-odd species has either the equipment or the inclination to prey on man, more people are injured by this curiously shaped creature than by all other fish combined.

The most dangerous of the rays is the venomous variety known as the stingray. It varies in shape from round to kite or diamond and in size from five inches to seven feet across. Stingrays are unaggressive but quite capable of defending themselves against any man or creature that intrudes on their habitat. Above its tail, in its envenomed stinger, the stingray (opposite) packs a formidable weapon. Bottom-dwellers, stingrays burrow in the mud or sand, and their natural camouflage makes them hard to see. Like many animals with a powerful defensive system, they are slow to move out of the way, perhaps taking it for granted that they will be left alone. When a stingray is disturbed, the results are nearly always disastrous for the intruder. The creature's spine, which has specialized venom-producing cells, is erected and the muscular tail is used to drive the spine into the victim's body. Teethlike serrations tear tissue and facilitate the spread of venom.

Although a few fatal encounters have been reported, nobody is sure what percentage of stingray injuries end in death because only a small number of victims are seen by a physician. The venomous creature abounds in all the seas of the world; there are also freshwater varieties that are as deadly as the saltwater-dwellers. The stingray, an ancient animal, has been known as a peril since Greco-Roman times. Pliny the Elder erroneously concluded that the ray used its sting to paralyze its prey. Ulysses is said to have been killed by a spear tipped with a stingray spine, and Captain John Smith was badly stung while fishing in Chesapeake Bay in 1608 but survived to eat the ray.

Another member of the raioid group is the nonvenomous skate, which so closely resembles the ray that fishermen and other frequenters of the sea tend to lump them together. Experts can tell the difference by their shape, skates generally having long noses that rays lack. Another cartilaginous fish closely related to both the shark and the ray is the sawfish, which, as the name implies, possesses a long saw-toothed snout with which it cuts and chops smaller fish to death for food. While extremely dangerous when handled, the sawfish is not known as a man-killer.

The biggest and most fearsome-looking of the rays is the giant manta, also called the devilfish in all the temperate-tropical regions it inhabits. The paradox of this huge and spectacular creature lies in the fact that for all its size and diabolic appearance it is unaggressive and rarely attacks anything larger than a shrimp. The only threat the manta poses to man is the remote possibility of its falling on him accidentally—or frightening him to death. The manta, which grows to a breadth of 20 to 25 feet and a weight of more than 3,000 pounds, lives near the surface of the sea and periodically emerges to indulge in a series of aerial leaps, jumping as high as 15 feet out of the water and crashing its enormous bulk back onto the waves with the explosive noise of a detonating bomb. At times the mantas will vary the performance, breaking water headfirst and then turning completely in a splashy cartwheel, one pectoral fin emerging as the other sinks back into the sea.

These spectacular acrobatics are motivated neither by sheer exuberance, as at times they seem to be, nor by the desire to scare prospective prey to death. One theory is that the leaping may be a territorial display, for the thunderous sound the manta makes when it crashes back into the sea after such a leap may serve as the ray's statement of claim to the area. The muscles that power such awesome calisthenics can also be set off by a harpoon. One specimen with a 22-foot wingspread is reported to have towed a 25-foot motorboat more than 10 miles with four harpoons and a half-dozen rifle bullets in its body. Similarly cruel treatment used to be accorded the manta by Mexican fishermen who entertained tourists by paddling a small cockleshell into position over one of the beasts, harpooning the manta and then flattening themselves in the boat for a high-speed, half-airborne trip over the waves.

Unlike most fish, the rays reproduce by physical union. One observer claims to have witnessed the mating of a pair of mantas off the North Carolina coast. "Copulation," he reported, "was not accomplished by vertical motion, but by a graceful serpentine lateral curvature of the spine," as the male alternately advanced one of his claspers while he withdrew the other. Occasionally the two separated, swam about in graceful leisurely curves or leaped lustily skyward. Manta young are reportedly born, sometimes at least, during the female's great leaps from the water and thus make their entry into life high in the air.

Hide and Hitch

An unwary bather stepping on a stingray half buried in the sand (left) or flattened out on a coral reef (above) is in for a painful surprise. Most rays are masters of melting into their background, but the giant manta (opposite) is highly visible as it moves majestically through shallow waters and under the ocean's surface, convoyed by groups of remoras, small fish that often attach themselves to the giant rays, hitchhiking to the next good feeding ground. Though mantas are nonaggressive, feeding only on plankton and small fish, they can become a hazard when harpooned or fouled in fishnets or during their great leaps into the air. Prudent bathers and fishermen avoid mantas as studiously as they sidestep their stinging and electrically charged cousins.

Flight of the Rays

Slowly moving their elongated, winglike pectoral fins and flanks as they swim gracefully just under the surface of the water, the spotted eagle rays (above) do indeed resemble large birds of prey. Spotted eagle rays are equipped with whiplike tails just behind their dorsal fins, which serve as rudders. They have hard snouts and powerful jaws that can easily crack the shells of clams and other mollusks on which they feed.

The spectacular leaps of a giant manta ray are shown in the filmstrip at right. Scientists theorize that these aerial acrobatics may be a manta's way of staking claim to its territory, or the jumps of a female going into labor, or perhaps a ray's efforts to shake loose the parasites that cling to its body.

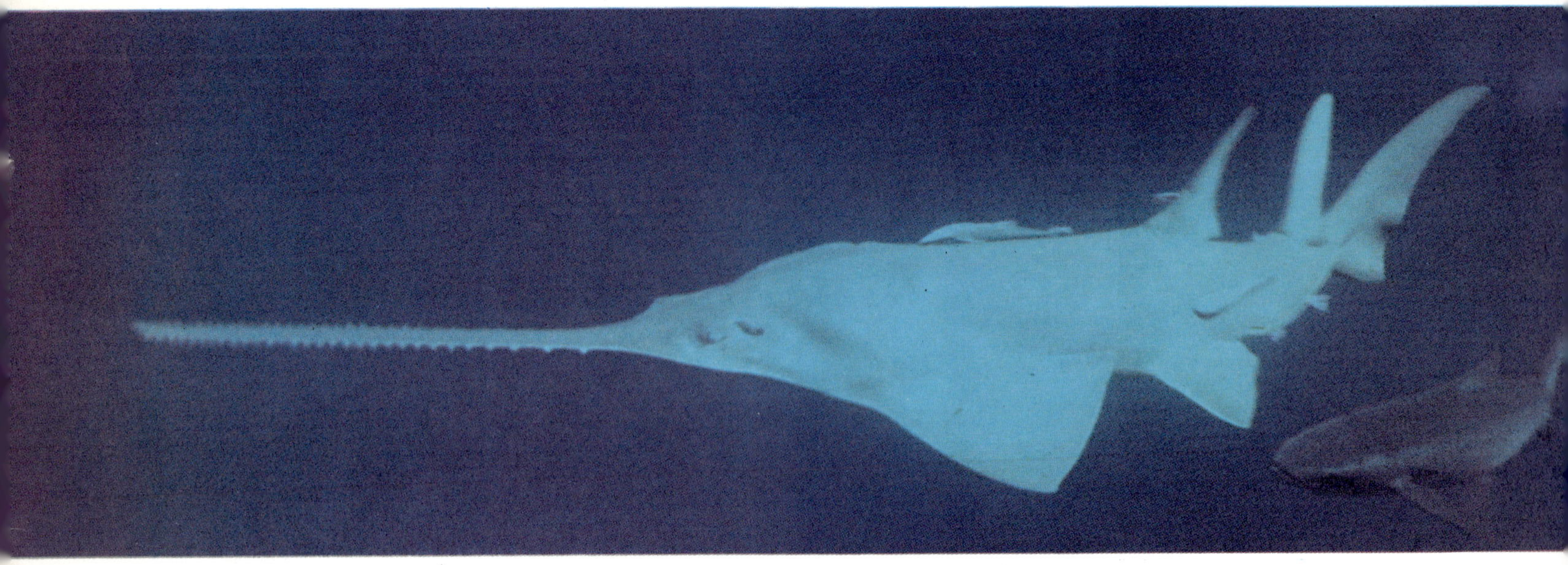

The formidable snout of a sawfish (above) is useful for slashing through schools of fish and disabling those on which it feeds.

The serrated teeth of the sawfish (left) are never a real danger to humans unless they are stepped on accidentally. Caught in a fisherman's net or loose on the deck of a boat, though, the ripsaw teeth present a considerable hazard.

En Garde

The order Rajiformes includes many curiously formed members, ranging in shape from kites to rhomboids to the bizarre, long-nosed—and dangerous-in-close-quarters—sawfish (left). The ruddy scrawled ray (right) is among the most common of the stingrays, an inhabitant of coral reefs. The thorny skate (above) is equipped with spiny protuberances on its back, which are dangerous only when a hapless bather treads on them.

Electric Rays and Eels

A bather venturing into the ocean or a river should be aware that a multitude of dangerous creatures is sharing the water with him and that, without appropriate care, he might be bitten by a barracuda, stung by a ray or a jellyfish, or even attacked by a shark. But he is not likely to realize that there is also a very real possibility of being stunned, even electrocuted, by a high-voltage shock deliberately emitted by bizarre aquatic creatures.

Yet that is exactly what can happen if a diver or bather gets too close to an electric ray (opposite) or an electric eel. Of all animals living on land and in water, apart from man, only fish can use electricity as a weapon. Although there are some 250 species that produce electrical charges—which they variously use to defend themselves, stun their prey, navigate and possibly to communicate on such essential subjects as food and sex—only the ray and the eel possess sufficient amperage to endanger man.

The electric ray, also known as the torpedo, is of the same flapjack-shape as its relatives, the stingray and the skate. It comes in a variety of sizes and voltages. The common *Torpedo torpedo* of the eastern Atlantic Ocean and the Mediterranean Sea rarely reaches a length of as much as two feet and puts out only 50 volts, enough to knock out or kill the smaller fish and crustaceans on which it feeds but not enough to affect man with anything more serious than a sharp tingle. At the other end of the power scale is the largest of the species, a creature called *Torpedo nobiliana*, which inhabits the Atlantic Ocean and the Mediterranean Sea, usually at depths of 200 feet but sometimes within wading distance of the shore. This six-foot, 200-pound dynamo can generate up to 200 volts, with a wattage output sufficient to stun a man who steps on it or happens to come close to it in the sea, since salt water is an excellent conductor of electricity.

Torpedo rays carry their power packs around with them at the base of the pectoral fins, where the muscles have been modified to form electrical plates with a negative underside and a positive topside. These electrical organs have developed at the expense of real muscle movement, so that the torpedo must propel itself mainly with its tail rather than its side fins. From the pectoral power pack nerve connections lead to the brain, which sends the order to shock or not to shock. Much of the creature's power potential is expended in the first sudden discharge, and the ray must rest and recharge after each attack.

Electric rays have been known to man for thousands of years. That ubiquitous scientific researcher Aristotle studied them and noted that they caught their prey by means of a stupefying apparatus that ejected "a sort of poison or elixir, yet being neither." Oppian of Corycus, a Greek poet of the second century A.D., observed that the ray "on a sudden would eject poisoned charm." The classical writers were understandably mystified, because electricity as such was unknown to them, and it was not until the work of Luigi Galvani in the late 18th century that scientists began to understand the electrochemical nature of the impulses that carry messages along the body's network of nerves. Simply stated, it is the utilization of this chemical process of generating electricity within the body that gives the torpedo ray its power to shock.

Electric eels generate their power in much the same way, although more of the eel's body is given over to the electricity-producing mechanism—about 75 percent—enabling the eel to crank up higher voltages than the ray. It thus represents more of a menace to man, particularly in the case of the biggest of the breed, a 10-foot freshwater giant native to South America called, with double emphasis on its chief distinguishing characteristic, *Electrophorus electricus* and capable of discharging a flash of 600 volts. Experts have measured eel discharges of 550 volts at just under two amperes, which means a shock output of about one kilowatt. In captivity, eels have been wired up to make light bulbs flash or to transmit the sounds of their varied frequencies through amplifiers hooked to loudspeakers. Electric eels have another curious characteristic that they share with some lizards: the ability to regenerate the rear parts of their bodies, including almost all of the elongated tail.

Electric eels are not true eels at all and deserve a separate classification of their own that they would share with other electricity-producing marine life. Besides the electric ray and numerous smaller fish, this category would include the electric catfish of Africa, which grows to a length of three or four feet. Known to the ancient Egyptians for its mysterious emanations, this catfish can deliver a substantial jolt but cannot electrocute a man.

Shock Troops of the High Seas

Long before the invention of the cattle prod or the electric chair, electric rays were effectively employing their unusual shocking ability to stun their enemies and electrocute their prey. Unlike most other shore-hugging rays, the shockers are at home in midocean, often at considerable depths. Their electricity-producing apparatus takes up much of their body. The electrical shock, which has been recorded at as much as 200 volts, is discharged by two large organs at the base of each pectoral fin. There are three main types—the torpedo ray (above), the eyed electric ray (left) and the blimplike marbled electric ray (below).

Electric Eels: Living High-tension Wires

The menacing creature above is distantly related to the common carp and the amiable goldfish. But the electric eel is no goldfish. In its sausagelike body it packs a natural generating system containing 6,000 electric cells, triggered by the eel's brain and capable of stunning a frog from a distance of three feet. Electric eels are American freshwater creatures, inhabiting still waters and sluggish streams from the Guyanas to Argentina. Their electrifying ability is shared only by the electric rays and two bony fish, the stargazer and an African catfish. Nocturnal hunters, they lie dormant by day. Their elongated bodies consist mostly of electric tissue. The pits visible on its head are electrosensory organs by means of which the eel can sense changes in the electric field it creates about itself, and thus it becomes aware of objects in its vicinity as well as the electric shocks of other eels.

Savage Fish

Scientists divide the vertebrate villains of the world's waters into two major classifications: cartilaginous—or those with backbones of gristle or cartilage, such as the shark and the ray—and bony, those with skeletons of true bone. Four of the latter, differing greatly in size and mode of attack but sharing the common characteristic of being capable of severely biting man, are the barracuda, certain eels, the giant grouper and the piranha (opposite).

Among the most dangerous of the bony fish is the barracuda, a killer whose attack is so swift that it is seldom seen, with the bloody and often fatal results sometimes being blamed on the shark. Barracuda attacks are rare, but when they do occur they often cripple their victims. They have long, lithe bodies—often hard to see approaching head on—and needle-sharp teeth that lend themselves to a hit-and-run technique. In tropical waters, off Florida and in the Caribbean, barracudas are often more feared than sharks.

The barracuda's bad name goes back to the early years of exploration of the New World. In 1665 Lord de Rochefort in his *Natural History of the Antilles* wrote: "Among the monsters greedy and desirous of human flesh, the Becune [a West Indian name for the barracuda] is one of the most formidable." Fatal attacks on humans by barracudas have been recorded from various parts of the world since 1884.

The eel family is particularly large and diversified. But one baffling trait is common to several species: an uncanny homing instinct. A Danish scientist, Dr. Johannes Schmidt, spent much of his life, from 1904 to 1933, researching the breeding habits of common European and American freshwater eels and proved that they migrate in the fall to that area of the Atlantic known as the Sargasso Sea, where they spawn and die. Mysteriously, their offspring make their way back to the rivers from which their parents came. For the European eel, this means a trip of about three years; for the American variety, the passage takes just under a year. Only two species are dangerous: the conger and the moray. The conger, which can grow to a length of eight feet and weigh up to 150 pounds, has powerful teeth and a bulldog bite. It will attack a man only when disturbed. Once it gets hold of an arm or leg, the only recourse is to cut off its head—and even then the jaws may have to be pried open. The moray has an even more evil reputation than the conger, which it exceeds in size and in voraciousness. The poet Horace reported that the ancient Romans, who like Mediterranean people of all centuries had a taste for moray meat, kept the beasts in special breeding tanks, feeding them the live bodies of recalcitrant slaves. Morays have sharp teeth and powerful jaws and have been known to attack man, although no authenticated fatalities have been recorded in modern times.

Until recently the giant grouper was dismissed as a torpid, timid creature to be avoided by man only because of its size, which was reckoned at a maximum weight of 700 pounds and a length of eight feet. Ichthyologists scoffed at a report published some years back by the reputable Australian daily, the Sydney *Morning Herald*, that the real reason for the disappearance of a number of Pacific pearl divers, who had been working at considerable depths in regulation diving suits, was that they had been swallowed whole by the big fish. But as diving equipment and techniques improved, allowing man to work at increasing depths, experts began to revise their evaluation of the grouper; and many now feel that the deeper man explores, the bigger the groupers grow. Deep-sea divers working on oil rigs in the Gulf of Mexico have reported mammoth groupers big enough, according to one imaginative eyewitness, "to swallow a Volkswagen."

The piranhas, like the one opposite, as every reader of adventure yarns knows, have the capacity to skeletonize a hapless victim in a matter of minutes. As in most fish stories, the legend of the piranha is based on fact, but the truth is not quite so gruesome as the fiction. There are more than 20 species, ranging in length from a few inches to a foot and a half, which inhabit rivers in an area of South America spreading over four million square miles. Most are harmless; only the black piranha and three close relatives constitute a danger to man. There is no question that if enough of them congregate around a man-size animal, they can strip it in short order. But although there are numerous authenticated reports of piranhas biting people, there are few verified human fatalities attributed to these little fish. This fact notwithstanding, the United States government has placed tight controls on the importation of piranhas, which have long been popular with home-aquarium enthusiasts. Some aficionados with fickle tastes have introduced the dangerous creatures to southern waterways by flushing them down toilets and throwing them in streams.

Piranhas and Barracudas: Formidable Killers

While the legends that surround barracudas (opposite, below) and piranhas (above) are more numerous than the known facts about them, there can be no doubt that the two are among the more dangerous aquatic creatures. Only four of the 20 species of piranhas will attack humans who intrude on the South American rivers they inhabit. But the needlelike teeth of these four can sever a chunk of flesh as cleanly as a scalpel. Though many humans have been wounded by piranhas and natives of the river basins where they live are terrified of them, there are few authenticated reports of the fish ever having killed a man. Yet, schools of the little fish have been known to skeletonize a 400-pound hog in minutes. The sight of a school of piranhas reducing some hapless animal to bones is not easily forgotten. Indians of South America use the jawbones of piranhas as cutting implements and call them "scissors."

Although some barracudas, because of their small size, are considered harmless, the larger forms, which can reach a length of six feet, are swift, vicious attackers. The dangerous, bony fish (bottom) are sometimes seen following divers by the hour. Although the chance of an encounter with a barracuda is rare, once bitten, there is a real danger of bleeding to death from the deep wounds inflicted by their teeth (below).

The Living Sea

by Jacques-Yves Cousteau

The undersea world is a mysterious one, filled with secrets, teeming with varied life forms. Jacques-Yves Cousteau, the world-famous undersea explorer, has unlocked some of the secrets of the sea and, through his books and his television programs, has given earthbound man a chance to investigate the wonders and terrors of the world's waters.

The excerpt below comes from The Living Sea, *a record of exploration carried on from Cousteau's ship* Calypso. *While anchored near Assumption Reef in the Indian Ocean, the crew of the* Calypso *discovers that the ship has inadvertently become the feeding grounds for the sinister barracuda.*

During our dreary decompression stops ten feet under *Calypso*, we noted a lone barracuda, about four feet long, that skulked on the outskirts, never coming near us. We also saw three dozen remoras that had clamped themselves on the stern quarters two thousand miles back when we killed their shark hosts. The suckerfish had apparently been living on *Calypso*'s garbage. We inventoried the remoras during stage decompression and learned that one or two of them left the ship each day. We wondered why. When a dozen suckerfish were left, Falco started diving at dawn to see why the remoras were leaving. His prowl was rewarded by something none of us had seen in thousands of hours underwater.

Falco came dripping to the breakfast table. "I saw the barracuda take a remora," he said. "I was a hundred feet away. The barracuda dashed to the stern and picked it off. I went in quickly. The barracuda had cut it in two and swallowed half. It had the other half crosswise in its mouth as it swam away." There it was: *Calypso* was providing bed and breakfast for a barracuda. We broke our truce on killing in the Aldabras. "Get your *arbalete*," I told Falco. He dived with his spear gun and executed the barracuda with a single shot.

There are three disturbing aspects of barracudas—their evil, threatening faces, their disagreeable habit of swimming close to your feet, and their gaudy reputation as man-eaters. The latter is merely an assumption based on the first attribute. Still . . . early in our work at Assumption, I was sixty feet down in the reef, filming close-ups of the guests in a fancy coral hotel. When the reel ran out, I gave the camera to my assistant to carry up while I used the rest of my air on a sightseeing ramble.

I turned away from him and looked at a wall of middle-sized barracudas. I looked up and down and to the sides through my diving mask, which limits vision like horse blinders. The bulkhead of barracudas extended from the ocean's floor to the surface. Alone and barehanded, I could not suppress a tremor of panic. We had never paid attention to barracudas, and I had dismissed them in print as being of no danger to divers. Now, in this confrontation, I was not so sure. They might have a mob psychology that would produce a sudden, irreparable act at any moment.

I told myself to stop being frightened and take refuge on the reef. I wheeled. A curtain of barracudas obscured the reef. With a hammering heart, I turned full around. I was encircled by wild animals, revolving deliberately around me, three or four fish thick. I could not see through them. There was no way out. I sank motionless to the bottom of the well, conserving the remainder of my air. The great silver cylinder turned evenly on the axis of my exhalations several times and then unrolled in a curtain of tail fins stroking west in the ocean.

The Menacing Morays

There are approximately 100 species of moray eels, most of which are found in and around the coral reefs of the world's tropical and subtropical waters. Scuba divers investigating these rocky coasts should be particularly wary of them since they curl up in the dark recesses of the coral and rock formations. Morays are generally not aggressive toward humans, but when they are provoked or threatened they will lash out aggressively at any intruder—fish or man—that comes within reach of the length of their bodies, which are often as long as eight feet, delivering a jagged though nonpoisonous bite that can be quite painful indeed. At night the eels come out of their rocky refuges to prey on small fish, crustaceans and even an occasional octopus. Despite their dangerous jaws and menacing appearance, and the fact that they are sometimes extremely poisonous to eat, morays are highly prized food fish in South America and Asia.

Big Mouth

The cavernous mouths of some groupers are capable of sucking in almost any marine creature, including such monsters as the giant sea turtles. Their huge jaws act as suction pumps that draw in any living creature in their path. Weighing in at as much as 1,000 pounds, they may be capable of swallowing a man in one gulp. The pearl divers of the Orient are justifiably afraid of these deep-sea predators, which lurk in the coral reefs and the sunken hulls of ships. Although there are no authenticated accounts of a grouper actually killing a human, many stories of narrow escapes, and the mysterious disappearances of divers, mark the grouper as a genuine menace of the deep.

Fish Out of Water

Blennies and needlefish have two things in common: Certain species of both are equipped with razor-sharp teeth, and some will, on occasion, emerge from the water. Blennies come in a dazzling array of colors, from gold to violet, and are masters of camouflage, like the seaweed-dwelling variety at left. Needlefish, like their cousins the flying fish, will soar out of the waves in long, looping lunges to escape their enemies.

Needlefish are especially feared by night divers—for example, Japanese lobstermen, who, when diving at night, use lights to which the needlefish are attracted. Many of these fishermen have been badly injured by stab wounds inflicted by giant needlefish and have grown to fear these creatures more than sharks.

The elongated saber-toothed blenny (above) has doglike teeth that can quickly shred the small fish and crustaceans that make up its principal diet, but at a length of only two inches it presents absolutely no danger to man. Blennies range the oceans from the tropics to the frigid coast of Norway, and several subspecies have adapted to freshwater lakes and rivers.

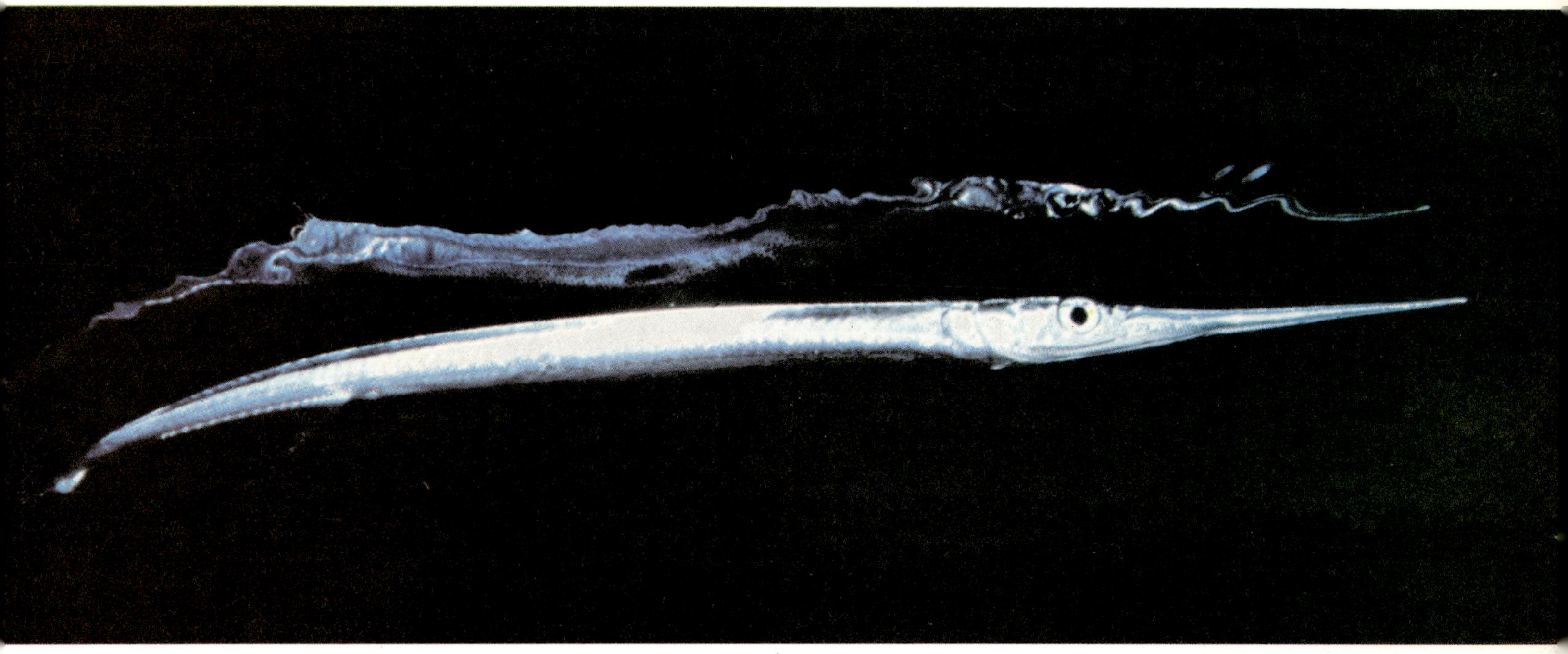

The rapier-snouted needlefish casts a reflected glow at night (above). It inhabits tropical and subtropical waters and travels in large schools, like the group at left, photographed in the tepid sea off Guam.

Poisonous and Venomous Fish

The family of scorpion fish includes several hundred species, some of them as venomous as a cobra, that inhabit tropical and subtropical waters. One species, the scorpion fish proper, is shown opposite. Another member of the family is the zebra fish, among the most strikingly marked of all coral-reef fish. Known in various parts of the world as the lion-fish, red fire-fish, tandan, butterfly cod, lolong and rock perch, its most appropriate pseudonym is that of turkey fish, derived from its habit of slowly swimming about with its fanlike pectorals and lacy dorsal fins extended like a gobbler strutting about a farmyard. Observers who succumb to the temptation to touch this majestic show-off are in for a painful surprise, for hidden beneath the spreading finery are 18 venomous spines that not only deliver a sometimes deadly poison but also have a nasty tendency to break off in the wound.

Still other marine creatures are dangerous to man, not because of envenomating powers but because they are poisonous if eaten. The most notorious are the puffer fish, some of which contain a nerve poison 150,000 times more potent than curare. Despite its proven deadliness, puffer is a favored fish flesh in Japan, where diners flock to restaurants specializing in *fugu*, as the puffer is called there. Fugu-eating is a popular fad even though it has been called the culinary equivalent of Russian roulette. About 10 Japanese die annually from eating the wrong parts of puffers. Fugu disciples say the flesh tastes like particularly good chicken, and the ingestion of *fugu* produces a mild intoxication with feelings of warmth and exhilaration. Undoubtedly it is this capacity to induce euphoria that attracts the patrons of the *fugu* palaces, even though they know they could be risking their lives with each mouthful. The Japanese government has taken steps to eliminate the danger of *fugu*-eating by requiring the licensing and training of *fugu* chefs in the proper preparation and cooking of the fish. In the United States one species of puffer, also known as the blowfish, appears on American tables under the appealing name of "sea squab."

The puffers, which get their name from their habit of inflating themselves by gulping large quantities of air or water, include several different species found in tropical and subtropical latitudes but in the greatest concentrations in Pacific waters. A near relative is the highly poisonous porcupine fish, which when threatened not only inflates itself with water into a balloon shape but also erects sharp quills all over its body.

There appear to be so many potentially lethal creatures in the shallows and the depths that unless one keeps firmly in mind that nearly all of them are nonaggressive and will almost always flee from man rather than attack him, the temptation to stay clear of the water altogether could become overpowering. Of the many major categories of venomous marine vertebrates, a few deserve special mention.

Outstanding among this group of relatively small but highly noxious poisoners are the weever fish. Dwellers on the sandy and muddy bay bottoms of the eastern Atlantic and the Mediterranean, weevers rarely exceed 18 inches in length but are among the most dangerous of all the bony fish. Their stings are extremely painful and may be fatal. Buried in the sediment, the weever is always ready to defend itself. Its armament is impressive, consisting of an erectile dorsal fin with long, bladelike spines, each with its own venom supply. The slightest disturbance of a weever can set off this multiple array of envenomating equipment. A weever wound produces instantaneous and severe pain that intensifies as the poison takes effect, attaining an excruciating peak within 30 minutes. Often morphine gives no relief. The pain subsides in a few hours and is followed by such symptoms as headache, fever, chills, nausea, respiratory distress, convulsions and sometimes death.

Toadfish are another nasty group of marine fish, characterized by broad, depressed heads and a generally ugly appearance. They inhabit many of the warm, calm waters of the world, and one species is found along the North American eastern seaboard. One species delivers its venom through four hollow, slender spines—one on either gill cover and the other two on the upper, or dorsal, fin. Wounds are painful but not fatal.

A far more dangerous creature is the stonefish, which is not only one of the world's most virulent animals but also one of the ugliest. Its back is covered with jagged, lethal spines and its entire body with unsightly warts. This rough covering permits it to envelop itself in slime, coral debris and algae, providing complete camouflage and increasing the chances of its being stepped on. Stonefish are most commonly encountered in Australian waters, where they have been blamed for fatalities among bathers who have died within hours of stepping on one.

A Bristling Menace

There are about 350 species of fish in the family Scorpaenidae (commonly called scorpion fish), many of which are venomous. These include the stonefish (below) and the rockfish (opposite, above). Many of the venomous scorpion fish live in tide pools and shallow areas of the world's tropical waters, where their protective coloring provides easy camouflage among the dappled coral reefs and rocky crevices. Depending on the species, scorpion fish have 17 or 18 venomous spines that are covered by a layer of skin called the integumentary sheath. As each spine enters the victim its sheath is pushed down, releasing the venom from the gland that lies hidden beneath it. Catfish have fewer spines than scorpion fish, but they are able to lock the spines defensively in place when they become agitated. All of the estimated 2,000 species of catfish have these sharp, stout protrusions, but only a few, such as the sea catfish (opposite, below), possess a venom capable of causing death. Catfish are primarily warm, freshwater dwellers that have smooth, scaleless bodies and long whiskerlike barbels around the mouth that function as feelers.

There are about 60 species of rockfish in the scorpion fish family, most of which are found in the cool and temperate waters of the Pacific. They have a hard protective covering around their heads as well as the needle-sharp spines common to all scorpion fish.

Sea catfish (left) often travel in schools in the Indian and Pacific oceans. Despite their small size (about 10 inches long), these catfish's poisonous fins mark them as dangerous inhabitants of tropical coral reefs.

Look but Don't Touch

The most exotic of all the scorpion fish are the stunningly striped zebra fish. When not hiding in rocky crevices the fish, which often travel in pairs, swim in the open with an unhurried grace, their featherlike fins swaying to and fro. Among those fins are hidden the zebra fish's 18 long, slender, pointed spines. They deliver a venom that, at first, results in a painful and swollen wound but that can later cause gangrene, delirium, convulsions, cardiac failure and even death. The zebra fish is found in the Red Sea and the Indian Ocean and in the waters around China, Japan and Australia. Swimmers in these areas should treat the zebra fish with caution and avoid approaching it closely, especially from the side. Such an approach agitates the fish, which reacts by moving around so that its dorsal spine is aimed directly at the intruder and, without warning, inflicts its harmful sting with a darting, lightning-fast jab.

The Swells of the Sea

The puffer fish (below and opposite) and the closely related porcupine fish (left) are highly poisonous marine animals that, when irritated, blow themselves up to three times their normal size by retaining water and air in their stomachs or in flexible abdominal sacs. Puffers have a strong sense of territoriality and seek rocky crevices into which they can retreat. When two puffers meet they often react by inflating themselves, flipping upside down and confronting each other belly to belly. Puffer fish have fleshy mouths and birdlike beaks, which they grind when inflating and deflating, making both extremely noisy processes. They feed primarily on hard-shelled crustaceans such as crabs, which they uproot by shooting a stream of water into the sandy sea floor through their puckered lips.

The Swift Surgeon, the Patient Toad

The surgeonfish (above, and opposite, below) of tropical waters have scalpel-sharp spines on either side of the base of their tail fins. These blades, which point forward, are normally recessed and partially covered by an integumentary sheath. But when the fish becomes excited it raises its spine at right angles to its body and, with a rapid, slashing motion of its tail, can inflict a deep and painful wound. Ichthyologists have not yet determined whether or not surgeonfish are venomous. There is no doubt, however, about some species of toadfish whose needle-sharp spines deliver a venom that, although not fatal, causes intense fever, pain and swelling. Toadfish inhabit the bottom of coastal waters of America, Europe, Africa and India. They hide in crevices or under rocks, or bury themselves in the muddy sands of the sea floor awaiting unwary prey. The eggs of the toadfish are spawned in the summer and are guarded by the male, who will give any intruder a vicious bite if disturbed while on duty. Toadfish venom, like that of all the venomous fish, is being studied by scientists for possible use in treating diseases.

A mottled toadfish (above) peeks out from its rocky hiding place. Toadfish are experts at camouflage and are able to change color at will to blend with their surroundings. The surgeonfish at left has its bright yellow, knifelike apparatus at the ready to ward off an unwelcome visitor.

Octopuses and Squids

Scientific names for the various families, classes and species of sea creatures are generally confusing to the layman, but the designation "cephalopods" for the group that includes the octopus and the squid is particularly apt. "Cephalopod" is derived from the Greek words for head and foot, and at a glance these many-tentacled predators seem to be all head and feet. Actually both have bodies housing the normal complement of internal organs, but because of the way they are built, it is difficult to decide where the head stops and the body starts. The distinctive characteristics are a multiplicity of tentacles (eight in the octopus and 10 in the squid), sharp beaks and remarkably humanoid, if somewhat sleepy-looking, eyes.

Octopuses and squid, which vary in size from less than an inch to at least 60 feet, have existed for probably 400 million years and are presently among the most abundant species in the sea. They have been the subject of imaginative writing for centuries. Homer wrote about the multipeds in wildly descriptive terms. Pliny the Elder reported on an octopus that was the scourge of Spanish fishermen, who set their dogs on the predator, provoking a battle royal in which the dogs came out the losers. Herman Melville in his masterpiece *Moby Dick* related the adventures of the crew of the whaling ship *Pequod* in an encounter with an enormous octopus, and in *Toilers of the Sea*, Victor Hugo wrote a terrifying account of the struggle between one man and an octopus (see page 76).

The class "Cephalopoda" includes at least one dangerous monster, the giant squid, and one vicious and venomous little creature called the blue-ringed octopus. The existence of the giant squid has been affirmed by seafaring men for centuries, and encounters with the huge predator have contributed to the building of many a sea-monster legend (see also page 114). But only within the past 100 years or so have scientists begun to accept it as a dangerous reality. A specimen that measured 57 feet, including its 35-foot-long tentacles, was washed up on a beach in New Zealand in 1888. There is evidence that much larger specimens live in the depths where they are unlikely to be encountered by man. Two 42-foot tentacles were vomited by a captive whale in an aquarium, and experts calculated that these had to belong to a monster measuring at least 66 feet and weighing better than 85,000 pounds.

The giant squid apparently attacks anything, pulling its prey with its long arms into position where its great parrot-like beak can tear it apart. Its archenemy is the sperm whale, one of the largest creatures on earth, which is preyed on by—and itself preys on—the big squid. This undoubtedly makes for some fierce deep-sea battles. Further evidence of the squid's unseen enormity is found on sperm whales that have survived battles with these behemoths: An ordinary giant squid of 50 feet leaves teeth-ringed sucker marks measuring between three and four inches across on a whale; but sperm whales have been captured with tentacle marks 18 inches across, which would have to have been inflicted by a gargantuan squid at least 200 feet long.

Science writer William J. Cromie, in his *Living World of the Sea*, calls the giant squid "the largest, swiftest and most terrifying invertebrate on Earth" and contends that the biggest of the breed "would make many of the fearsome dinosaurs of prehistory look like underfed alley cats." Whatever its proportions, the giant squid has a known record as a man-eater. When a British troopship went down in the Atlantic in March 1941, Cromie reports, "one survivor clinging to the life raft felt something grab his leg. While a dozen of his shipmates looked on in helpless horror, a great squid wrapped its tentacles around the sailor and pulled him screaming to his death."

Octopuses like the one opposite may attain a tentacle span of as much as 25 feet, and many species are big and powerful enough to hold a man under water until he drowns. The octopus, which reaches the zenith of intelligence among invertebrates, is solitary by nature and tends to avoid man rather than prey on him. It is equally clear that many, if not most, of the breed possess an envenomating capacity that they use for defense and to stun prey. Venom is contained in the salivary glands and is injected into a victim by means of the sharp beak. Depending on the species, the result may be anything from a minor localized irritation to paralysis and even death. The size of the cephalopod appears to have nothing to do with its deadliness. The two known fatalities from octopus bites, both of which occurred in Australia, are attributed to a small rock-dweller generally known as the blue-ringed octopus, which is only four inches in length. In both cases the victims were dead of respiratory failure within two hours of being bitten. The species also has been implicated in half a dozen other attacks on humans in which the victims suffered partial or total paralysis but recovered.

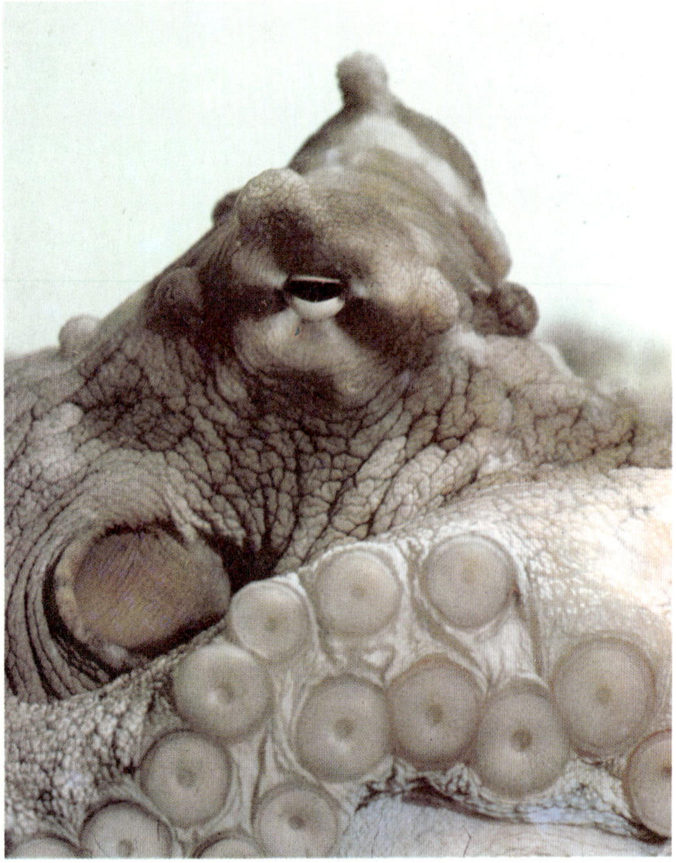

Eight-armed Loner

Octopuses prey on crustaceans, fish and mollusks, which they grab with their eight sucker-lined arms (above) and bite with their birdlike jaws, the only bony part of their body. Octopuses in turn are eaten by sperm whales and sharks. When they are attacked, the writhing creatures escape by changing color and obscuring themselves in an inky cloud. They are wary, solitary animals and congregate only during the brief mating period. The female octopus lays as many as 150,000 eggs, which cling together in grapelike clusters. The mother cleans and guards them ceaselessly during the weeks-long brooding period. During her vigil she doesn't even take time out to feed herself and usually dies after the eggs are hatched. Except for the venomous little blue-ringed octopus, a known killer, the major threat octopuses pose is to divers, who may be held underwater by the pull of even a small octopus.

A threatened male octopus (right) inflates himself to full size and pales to an opalescent white when his territory in an aquarium tank is invaded by a distinctively spotted night octopus (left).

Toilers of the Sea *by Victor Hugo*

To express his opposition to Louis Napolean's establishment of the Second Empire, Victor Hugo (1802–1885), one of France's foremost novelists and political activists, exiled himself to Jersey and then to Guernsey in the Channel Islands. It was on Guernsey in 1866 that he wrote Toilers of the Sea, *a novel that, with* Notre Dame de Paris *and* Les Misérables, *is considered among his most important works.*

The owner of a sunken steamboat, anxious to retrieve its valuable engine, offers the hand of his beautiful daughter as a reward to the man who accomplishes this seemingly impossible task. Gilliatt, a poor fisherman, accepts the challenge. One day, in pursuit of his mission, Gilliatt enters an underwater grotto and meets a formidable opponent.

He had made his way again into the singular cavern which he had visited in the previous month. The only difference was that he had entered by the way of the sea.

It was through the submarine arch which he had remarked before that he had just entered. At certain low tides it was accessible.

His eyes became more accustomed to the place; his vision became clearer and clearer; he was astonished. He found himself again in that extraordinary palace of shadows; saw again before his eyes that vaulted roof, those columns, those purple and blood-like stains, that vegetation rich with gems, and at the farther end that crypt or sanctuary and that altar-like stone. He took little notice of these details, but their impression was in his mind, and he saw that the place was unchanged.

He observed before him, at a certain height in the wall, the crevice through which he had penetrated the first time, and which from the point where he now stood appeared inaccessible.

Near the moulded arch he remarked those low dark grottos—a sort of caves within the cavern—which he had already observed from a distance. He now stood nearer to them. The entrance to the nearest to him was out of the water, and easily approachable. Nearer still than this recess he noticed, above the level of the water, and within reach of his hand, a horizontal fissure. It seemed to him probable that the crab had taken refuge there, and he plunged his hand in as far as he was able, and groped about in that dusky aperture.

Suddenly he felt himself seized by the arm. A strange indescribable horror thrilled through him.

Some living thing, thin, rough, flat, cold, slimy, had twisted itself round his naked arm in the dark depth below. It crept upward towards his chest. Its pressure was like a tightening cord, its steady persistence like that of a screw. In less than a moment some mysterious spiral form had passed round his wrist and elbow, and had reached his shoulder. A sharp point penetrated beneath the armpit.

Gilliatt recoiled, but he had scarcely power to move. He was, as it were, nailed to the place. With his left hand, which was disengaged, he seized his knife, which he still held between his teeth, and with that hand, holding the knife, he supported himself against the rocks, while he made a desperate effort to withdraw his arm. He succeeded only in disturbing his persecutor, which wound itself still tighter. It was supple as leather, strong as steel, cold as night.

A second form, sharp, elongated, and narrow, issued out of the crevice, like a tongue out of monstrous jaws. It seemed to lick his naked body. Then suddenly stretching out it became longer and thinner as it crept over his skin and wound itself round him. At the same time a terrible sense of pain, comparable to nothing he had ever known, compelled all his muscles to contract. He felt upon his skin a number of flat rounded points. It seemed as if innumerable suckers had fastened to his flesh and were about to drink his blood.

A third long undulating shape issued from the hole in the rock, seemed to feel its way about his body, lashed round his ribs like a cord, and fixed itself there.

Agony when at its height is mute. Gilliatt uttered no cry. There was sufficient light for him to see the repulsive forms which had entangled themselves about him. A fourth ligature, but this one swift as an arrow, darted towards his stomach and wound around him there.

It was impossible to sever or tear away the slimy bands which were twisted tightly round his body, and were adhering by a number of points. Each of the points was the focus of frightful and singular pangs. It was as if numberless small mouths were devouring him at the same time.

A fifth long, slimy, ribbon-shaped strip issued from the hole. It passed over the others, and wound itself tightly around his chest. The compression increased his sufferings. He could scarcely breathe.

These living thongs were pointed at their extremities, but broadened like the blade of a sword towards its hilt. All belonged evidently to the same centre. They crept and glided about him; he felt the strange points of pressure, which seemed to him like mouths, change their places from time to time.

Suddenly a large, round, flattened, glutinous mass issued from beneath the crevice. It was the centre; the five thongs were attached to it like spokes to the hub of a wheel. On the opposite side of this disgusting monster appeared the commencement of three other tentacles, the ends of which remained under the rock. In the middle of this slimy mass appeared two eyes.

The eyes were fixed on Gilliatt.

He recognized the devil-fish. . . .

It is difficult for those who have not seen it to believe in the existence of the devil-fish. Compared to this creature, the ancient hydras are insignificant.

At times we are tempted to imagine that the vague forms which float in our dreams may encounter in the realm of the Possible attractive forces, having power to fix their lineaments, and shape living beings, out of these creatures of our slumbers. The Unknown has power over these strange visions, and out of them composes monsters. Orpheus, Homer, and Hesiod imagined only the Chimera: God has created the devil-fish.

The Divine Will sometimes excels in monstrous forms

of life. The wherefore of this perplexes and affrights the religious thinker.

If terror were the object of its creation, nothing could be imagined more ideally perfect than the devil-fish.

The whale has enormous bulk, the devil-fish is comparatively small; the hippopotamus has its cuirass, the devil-fish is destitute of one; the jararaca makes a hissing noise, the devil-fish is mute; the rhinoceros has a horn, the devil-fish has none; the scorpion has a dart, the devil-fish has no dart; the *buthus* has claws, the devil-fish has none; the monkey has a prehensile tail, the devil-fish has no tail; the shark has sharp fins, the devil-fish has no fins; the vespertilio-bat has wings with claws, the devil-fish has no wings; the porcupine has his spines, the devil-fish has no spines; the sword-fish has his sword, the devil-fish has none; the torpedo has its electric spark, the devil-fish has none; the toad has its poison, the devil-fish has none; the viper has its venom, the devil-fish has no venom; the lion has its claws, the devil-fish has no claws; the griffon has its beak, the devil-fish has no beak; the crocodile has its jaws, the devil-fish has no teeth.

The devil-fish has no muscular organization, no menacing cry, no breastplate, no horn, no dart, no claw, no tail with which to hold or bruise, no cutting fins, no wings with nails, no prickles, no sword, no electric discharge, no poison, no talons, no beak, no teeth,—yet he is of all creatures the most formidably armed.

What then is the devil-fish? It is the sea vampire.

The swimmer who, attracted by the beauty of the spot, ventures among breakers in the open sea, where the still waters hide the splendors of the deep, or in the hollows of unfrequented rocks, in unknown caverns abounding in sea plants, testacea, and crustacea, under the deep portals of the ocean, runs the risk of meeting it. If that fate should be yours, be not curious, but fly. The intruder enters there dazzled, but quits the spot in terror.

This frightful apparition, which is always possible among the rocks in the open sea, is a grayish form which undulates in the water. It is of the thickness of a man's arm, and in length nearly five feet. Its outline is ragged. Its form resembles an umbrella closed, and without handle. This irregular mass advances slowly towards you. Suddenly it opens, and eight radii issue abruptly from around a face with two eyes. These radii are alive: their undulation is like lambent flames; they resemble, when opened, the spokes of a wheel of four or five feet in diameter,—a terrible expansion! It springs upon its prey.

The devil-fish lassoes its victim.

It winds around the sufferer, covering and entangling him in its long folds. Underneath it is yellow; above, of a dull, earthy hue: nothing could render that inexplicable shade dust-colored; from its color, this dweller of the sea might have been made of ashes. Its form is spider-like, but its tints are like those of the chameleon. When irritated it becomes violet. Its most horrible characteristic is its softness.

Its folds strangle, its contact paralyzes.

It has an aspect like gangrened or scabrous flesh. It is a monstrous embodiment of disease. . . .

Such was the creature into whose power Gilliatt had fallen for some minutes.

The monster was the inhabitant of the grotto, the terrible genius of the place,—a kind of sombre demon of the water.

All the splendors of the cavern existed for it alone.

On the day of the previous month when Gilliatt had first penetrated into the grotto, the dark outline vaguely per-

ceived by him in the ripples of the secret waters was this monster. It was here in its home.

When, entering for the second time into the cavern in pursuit of the crab, he had observed the crevice in which he supposed that the crab had taken refuge, the devil-fish was there lying in wait for prey.

Is it possible to imagine that secret ambush?

No bird would brood, no egg would burst to life, no flower would dare to open, no breast to give milk, no heart to love, no spirit to soar, under the influence of that apparition of evil watching with sinister patience in the dusk.

Gilliatt had thrust his arm deep into the opening; the monster had snapped at it. It held him fast, as the spider holds the fly.

He was in the water up to his belt, his naked feet clutching the slippery roundness of the huge stones at the bottom, his right arm bound and rendered powerless by the flat coils of the long tentacles of the creature, and his body almost hidden under the folds and cross-folds of this horrible bandage.

Of the eight arms of the devil-fish, three adhered to the rock, while five encircled Gilliatt. In this way, clinging to the granite on the one hand, and with the other to its human prey, it enchained him to the rock. Two hundred and fifty suckers were upon him, tormenting him with agony and loathing. He was grasped by gigantic hands, the fingers of which were each nearly a yard long, and furnished inside with living blisters eating into the flesh.

As we have said, it is impossible to tear oneself from the folds of the devil-fish. The attempt ends only in a firmer grasp. The monster clings with more determined force. Its effort increases with that of its victim; every struggle produces a tightening of its ligatures.

Gilliatt had but one resource,—his knife.

His left hand only was free, but the reader knows with what power he could use it. It might have been said that he had two right hands.

His open knife was in his hand.

The antennae of the devil-fish cannot be cut; they form a leathery substance, impossible to divide with the knife; it slips under the edge; its position in attack also is such that to cut it would be to wound the victim's own flesh.

The creature is formidable, but there is a way of resisting it. The fishermen of Sark know this, as does any one who has seen them execute certain abrupt movements in the sea. The porpoises know it also. They have a way of biting the cuttle-fish which decapitates it. Hence the frequent sight on the sea of pen-fish, polyps, and cuttle-fish without heads.

The polyp, in fact, is only vulnerable through the head.

Gilliatt was not ignorant of this fact.

He had never seen a devil-fish of this size. His first encounter was with one of the larger species. Another would have been powerless with terror.

With the devil-fish, as with a furious bull, there is a certain moment in the conflict which must be seized. It is the instant when the bull lowers the neck; it is the instant when the devil-fish advances its head. The movement is rapid. He who loses that moment is destroyed.

The things we have described occupied only a few moments. Gilliatt, however, felt the increasing power of two hundred and fifty suckers.

The monster is cunning; it tries first to stupefy its prey. It seizes and then pauses awhile.

Gilliatt grasped his knife; the sucking increased.

He looked at the monster, which seemed to look at him.

Suddenly it loosened from the rock its sixth antenna, and darting it at him, seized him by the left arm.

At the same moment it advanced its head with a violent movement. In one second more its mouth would have fastened on his breast. Bleeding in the sides, and with his two arms entangled, he would have been a dead man.

But Gilliatt was watchful. He avoided the antenna, and at the moment when the monster darted forward to fasten on his breast, he struck it with the knife clenched in his left hand. There were two convulsions in opposite directions: that of the devil-fish and that of its prey. The movement was rapid as a double flash of lightnings.

He had plunged the blade of his knife into the flat slimy substance, and by a rapid movement, like the flourish of a whip in the air, describing a circle round the two eyes, he wrenched the head off as a man would draw a tooth.

The struggle was ended. The folds relaxed. The monster dropped away, like the slow detaching of bands. The four hundred suckers, deprived of their sustaining power, dropped at once from the man and the rock. The mass sank to the bottom of the water.

Breathless with the struggle, Gilliatt could perceive upon the stones at his feet two shapeless, slimy heaps, the head on one side, the remains of the monster on the other,—for it could not be called a body.

Fearing, nevertheless, some convulsive return of his agony, he recoiled to avoid the reach of the dreaded tentacles.

But the monster was quite dead.

Gilliatt closed his knife.

The Skittish Squid

There are about 300 species of squids, two of which are seen here. All are saltwater dwellers, and all are predatory, feeding mainly on mollusks, fish, crustaceans and even on their own young. Squids seize their prey with any or all of their ten tentacles. Two of these arms are longer than the others and have paddle-shaped tips, but all ten appendages are studded with suckers and are formidable grabbing devices. When they are being pursued, squids eject an inky smoke screen that, combined with their remarkable ability to change color instantaneously, distracts the foe long enough for the squids to make a safe escape. Most squids have streamlined, torpedo-shaped bodies perfect for long-distance swimming. They propel themselves by taking in water (which also provides their oxygen) and then forcing it out of their bodies through a siphon. By increasing the pressure of this force, squids have been seen to dart away at speeds of up to 20 miles per hour.

Blushing Courtship

Despite their numerous enemies, ranging from the sperm whale to the mackerel, squids are among the most abundant of the larger sea creatures. Inhabiting every ocean, they ensure the survival of their species by producing enormous numbers of eggs. In the spring and summer, males seek out females and indulge in a brief courtship rite that involves a lot of arm-waving and color changes (such as the reddened tentacles of the mating squids at right). The male then passes packets of sperm to the female, who stores them until spawning time. The eggs are laid in transparent, gelatinous capsules (like those emerging from the mother squid above), which the female anchors with threadlike strings to rocks or shells. Unlike the female octopus, who guards her eggs to the death, squids leave their eggs unattended. The young of most shore squids are born looking like small replicas of their parents, while those spawned in the deep sea hatch as larvae that undergo further development as they mature.

As each buoyant pod of eggs is delivered (above), the female attaches it to the ones already spawned, forming a cluster of capsules called a mop (below). Other females sometimes add their strands to the cluster, forming a kind of communal nursery. Each pod contains up to 100 eggs, which take from 10 days to one month to hatch. The unguarded eggs often fall prey to other marine creatures, such as the sea urchins seen feeding on them below.

Poisonous and Venomous Invertebrates

The world of the coelenterates—as the spineless sea creatures such as jellyfish, corals, hydroids and sea anemones are called—is a strange one. Many of the coelenterates look more like plants than animals and rival the most exotic flowers in delicacy and color. And although equipped with some of the most efficient death-dealing apparatus in the sea, they do not attack, in the sense that a true predator such as a shark does, but lie in wait for their prey, their envenomed appendages at the ready to cause injury or death to anything careless enough to get within range.

The coelenterate most familiar to man is the jellyfish. Like the phosphorescent *Pelagia*, opposite, jellyfish are free-floating creatures consisting of a gelatinous, bell-shaped and almost invisibly transparent body from which armored tentacles trail. Although its composition is 90 percent water and it rapidly disintegrates when taken from the sea, the jellyfish is a living, functioning animal in its own element. It can propel itself by making a series of pulsating movements and is able to fish very effectively for its food and to reproduce its kind. Its tentacles are equipped with stinging cells called nematocysts that can best be likened to miniature hypodermic syringes.

Jellyfish, also known in some areas as sea nettles, are found in all the oceans of the world and range in size from a common nine-inch North American variety to an Arctic monster measuring eight feet across its umbrella-like main portion. All have a venomous potential and should be given a wide berth because of the radius of their tentacles, which in a medium-size jellyfish may trail out or down in the water for several feet. The giant Arctic species have stinging trailers extending an estimated 100 feet. Tactile encounters with any jellyfish are sure to produce in humans at least a painful and annoying skin rash and at worst an agonizing death. The most venomous of the jellyfish is the sea wasp, also called the box-jelly, a small and delicate blob of living matter found in the Indo-Pacific region, especially in the shallow waters off Australian beaches. The sea wasp's venom is so potent that once it enters the human bloodstream in sufficient quantity it can paralyze the heart in minutes.

The best known of what wary people think of as a jellyfish is the Portuguese man-of-war, so named because of the beautiful but ominous floating portion that appears above the surface of the sea and resembles the rigging of a caravel. It is widely distributed in temperate and tropical waters and has threadlike poisonous tentacles that may extend from the central float bag for 50 feet or more. The odd thing about the Portuguese man-of-war and what distinguishes it from the true jellyfish is that it is not an individual creature at all but a complex collection of many individuals with widely different functions. Each of the separate small animals has an assigned task. There are those that direct the movement of the whole complex, those that catch food, those that paralyze the prey and those that digest it and distribute the resulting nourishment throughout the entire aggregation. The Portuguese man-of-war might be likened to a Utopian community in which each individual performs the duties for which it is best suited and receives the rewards it needs.

Among the other coelenterates are the sea anemones, beautiful flowerlike but carnivorous creatures that affix themselves to rocks or the sea floor and wave their delicate but venomous tentacle-petals invitingly until a fish swims by to investigate, whereupon the deadly petals close on the prey, paralyzing it, and the central calyxlike mouth consumes it. Equally dangerous is the stinging coral, a tiny polyplike animal that lives in colonies and stings its prey. Like members of the coral family, when stinging corals die they leave behind their rock-hard and varicolored protective coating that is the building block for reefs.

There are also dozens of noncoelenterate but dangerous invertebrates such as the crown-of-thorns sea star with multiple tiny barbs, each mildly poisonous when touched; the spiny sea urchins, some of which have the unusual ability to leave their pincerlike pedicellariae lodged in the skin of their victims, where they continue to introduce venom until they are removed; and the annelids, or jointed worms, some of which can inflict a painful "O"-shaped bite that is often exacerbated by a coating of venom. Then there are the highly toxic and piscivorous cone shells, so tempting to the collector in their variegated color and design but containing a nasty little occupant with a treacherous and painful sting. The cone shells are tiny members of the enormous family of mollusks, the largest of which, the giant clam, measures five feet across and weighs up to 500 pounds. Divers have been reported temporarily trapped by the viselike grip of this big mollusk. However, no recorded fatality has ever been scored against it.

Beauties to Beware

Few forms of marine life are more beautiful than the gossamer jellyfish. Drifting gracefully across a tranquil sea, they appear to be as harmless as a blob of foam, and yet the merest touch of the tentacles of some species can inflict irritating welts on an unsuspecting swimmer. And when they invade the waters of bathing beaches in swarms of tens of thousands, as they sometimes do (below), jellyfish can transform the sea into a maritime minefield.

The Cyanea capillata, or lion's mane jellyfish (right), is the giant of all the species of jellyfish. Its belled sac reportedly measures eight feet or more across, while its tangle of poisonous tentacles, which are arranged in eight groups, each group having 150 tentacles, may reach over 100 feet in length. The lion's mane ranges widely in the Atlantic and Pacific oceans, and although it is not believed capable of killing an organism as large as a man, its sting can cause severe discomfort. The slightly venomous moon jellyfish (below) is found in all warm and temperate waters and is among the commonest members of the family.

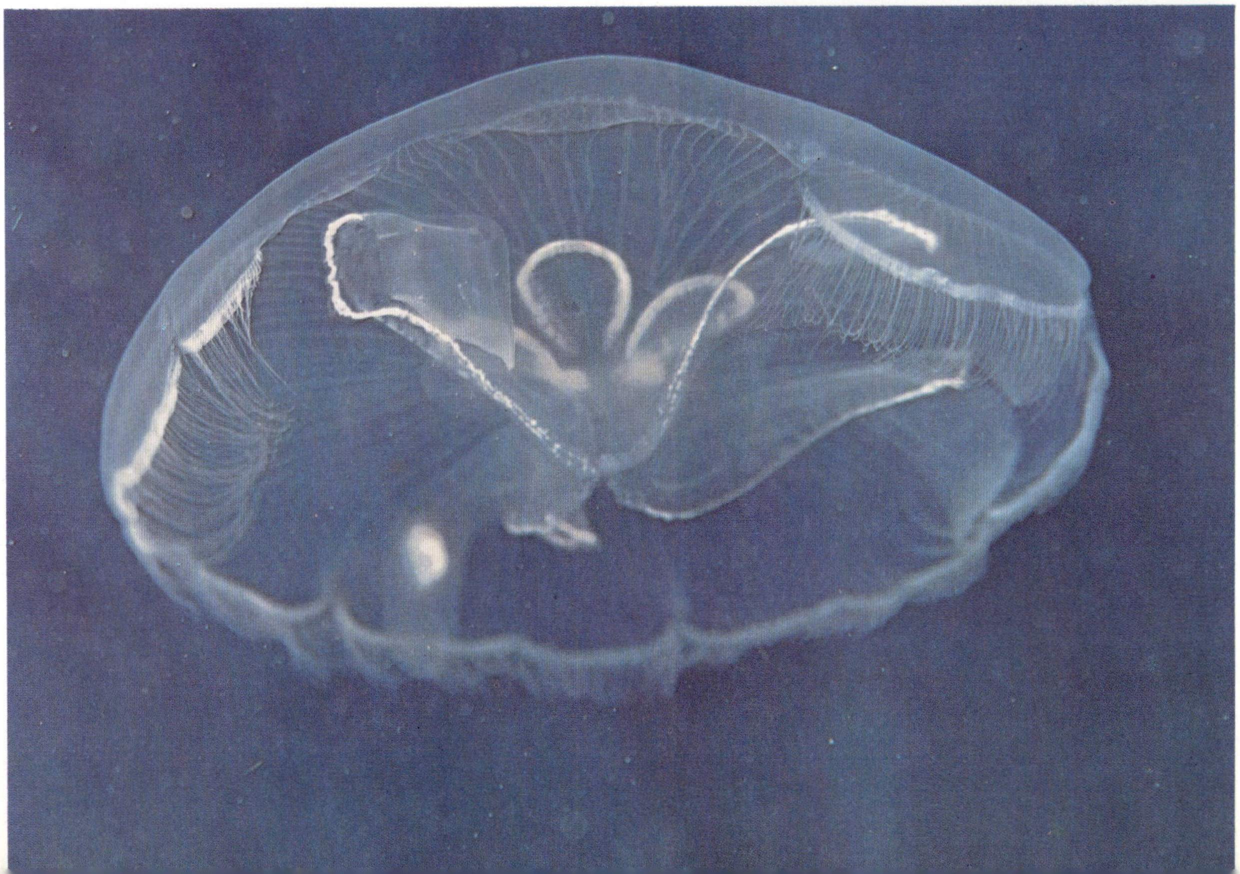

Pulsing eerily through the azure twilight of a tropic sea, the jellyfish at left seems like some giant from the abysmal depths; actually, it measures just five inches in diameter. Its tiny escorts huddle close for protection against predators.

THE EDGE OF

"The place of our dim ancestral beginning," believes Rachel Carson, is where the sea and shore meet. This place, teeming with fascinating creatures struggling for survival, is the subject of her book The Edge of the Sea, *from which the following excerpts are taken. Miss Carson (1907–1964), also the author of* The Silent Spring, Under the Sea Wind *and* The Sea Around Us, *was a marine biologist for the United States Fish and Wildlife Service for several years and later was that organization's editor-in-chief. In the selections below she tells of her encounters with the great red jellyfish along the rocky shores north of Cape Cod, with a fleet of Portuguese men-of-war on the sandy shores of the mid-Atlantic coast and with the black and rock-boring sea urchins along the coral coast of Florida.*

The great red jellyfish, Cyanea . . . in its periodic invasions of bays and harbors links the shallow green waters with the bright distances of the open sea. On fishing banks a hundred or more miles offshore one may see its immense bulk drifting at the surface as it swims lazily, its tentacles sometimes trailing for fifty feet or more. These tentacles spell danger for almost all sea creatures in their path and even for human beings, so powerful is the sting. Yet young cod, haddock, and sometimes other fishes adopt the great jellyfish as a "nurse," traveling through the shelterless sea under the protection of this large creature and somehow unharmed by the nettle-like stings of the tentacles.

THE SEA *by Rachel Carson*

Like Aurelia, the red jellyfish is an animal only of the summer seas, for whom the autumnal storms bring the end of life. Its offspring are the winter plantlike generation, duplicating in almost every detail the life history of the moon jelly. On bottoms no more than two hundred feet deep (and usually much less), little half-inch wisps of living tissue represent the heritage of the immense red jellyfish. They can survive the cold and the storms that the larger summer generation cannot endure; when the warmth of spring begins to dissipate the icy cold of the winter sea they will bud off the tiny discs that, by some inexplicable magic of development, grow in a single season into the adult jellyfish . . .

A whole fleet of Portuguese men-of-war is sometimes seen from vessels crossing the Gulf Stream when some peculiarity of the wind and current pattern has brought together a number of them. Then one can sail for hours or days with always some of the siphonophores in sight. With the float or sail set diagonally across its base, the creature sails before the wind; looking down into the clear water one can see the tentacles trailing far below the float. The Portuguese man-of-war is like a small fishing boat trailing a drift net, but its "net" is more nearly like a group of high-voltage wires, so deadly is the sting of the tentacles to almost any fish or other small animal unlucky enough to encounter them.

The true nature of the man-of-war is difficult to grasp, and indeed many aspects of its biology are unknown. But, as with Velella, the central fact is that what appears to be one animal is really a colony of many different individuals, although no one of them could exist independently. The float and its base are thought to be one individual; each of the long trailing tentacles another. The food-capturing tentacles, which in a large specimen may extend down for 40 or 50 feet, are thickly studded with nematocysts or stinging cells. Because of the toxin injected by these cells, Physalia is the most dangerous of all the coelenterates.

For the human bather, even glancing contact with one of the tentacles produces a fiery welt; anyone heavily stung is fortunate to survive. The exact nature of the poison is unknown. Some people believe there are three toxins involved, one producing paralysis of the nervous system, another affecting respiration, the third resulting in extreme prostration and death, if a large dose is received. In areas where Physalia is abundant, bathers have learned to respect it. On some parts of the Florida coast the Gulf Stream passes so close inshore that many of these coelenterates are borne in toward the beaches by onshore winds. The Coast Guard at Lauderdale-by-the-Sea and other such places, when posting reports of tides and water temperatures, often includes forecasts of the relative number of Physalias to be expected inshore.

Because of the highly toxic nature of the nematocyst poisons, it is extraordinary to find a creature that apparently is unharmed by them. This is the small fish Nomeus, which lives always in the shadow of a Physalia. It has never been found in any other situation. It darts in and out among the tentacles with seeming impunity, presumably finding among them a refuge from enemies. In return, it probably lures other fish within range of the man-of-war. But what of its own safety? Is it actually immune to the poisons? Or does it live an incredibly hazardous life? A Japanese investigator reported years ago that Nomeus actually nibbles away bits of the stinging tentacles, perhaps in this way subjecting itself to minute doses of the poison throughout its life and so acquiring immunity. But some recent workers contend that the fish has no immunity whatever, and that every live Nomeus is simply a very lucky fish.

The sail, or float, of a Portuguese man-of-war is filled with gas secreted by the so-called gas gland. The gas is largely nitrogen (85 to 91 per cent) with a small amount of oxygen and a trace of argon. Although some siphonophores can deflate the air sac and sink into deep water if the surface is rough, Physalia apparently cannot. However, it does have some control over the position and degree of expansion of the sac. I once had a graphic demonstration of this when I found a medium-size man-of-war stranded on a South Carolina beach. After keeping it overnight in a bucket of salt water, I attempted to return it to the sea. The tide was ebbing; I waded out into the chilly March water, keeping the Physalia in its bucket out of respect for its stinging abilities, then hurled it as far into the sea as I could. Over and over, the incoming waves caught it and returned it to the shallows. Sometimes with my help, sometimes without, it would manage to take off again, visibly adjusting the shape and position of the sail as it scudded along before the wind, which was blowing out of the south, straight up the beach. Sometimes it could successfully ride over an incoming wave; sometimes it would be caught and hustled and bumped along through thinning waters. But whether in difficulty or enjoying momentary success, there was nothing passive in the attitude of the creature. There was, instead, a strong illusion of sentience. This was no helpless bit of flotsam, but a living creature exerting every means at its disposal to control its fate. When I last saw it, a small blue sail far up the beach, it was pointed out to sea, waiting for the moment it could take off again. . . .

The edge of the low tide is a dark line traced by colonies of short-spined, rock-boring sea urchins. Every hole and every depression in the coral rock bristles with their small dark bodies. One spot in the Keys lives in my memory as an urchin paradise. This is the seaward shore of one of the eastern group of islands, where the rock drops in an abrupt terrace, somewhat undercut and deeply eroded into holes and small caves, many with their roofs open to the sky. I have stood on the dry rock above the tide and looked down into these little water-floored, rock-walled grottoes, finding twenty-five to thirty urchins in one of these caverns that was no larger than a bushel basket. The caves shine with a green water-light in the sun, and in this light the globular bodies of the urchins have a reddish color of glowing, luminous quality, in rich contrast to the black spines.

A little beyond this spot the sea bottom slopes under water more gradually, with no undercutting. Here the rock borers seem to have taken over every niche that can afford shelter; they give the illusion of shadows beside each small irregularity of bottom. It is not certain whether they use the five short stout teeth on their under surfaces to scrape out holes in the rock, or perhaps merely take advantage of natural depressions to find a safe anchorage against the occasional storms that sweep this coast. For some inscrutable reason, these rock-boring urchins and related species in other parts of the world are bound to this particular tidal level, linked to it precisely and mysteriously by invisible ties that prevent their wandering farther out over the reef flat, although other species of urchins are abundant there. . . .

Out on the reefs the long-spined black sea urchin excavates cavities along the base of the coral wall; each sinks into its depression and turns its spines outward, so that a swimmer moving along the reef sees forests of black quills. This urchin also wanders in over the reef flats, where it nestles close to the base of a loggerhead sponge, or sometimes, apparently finding no need of concealment, rests in open, sand-floored areas.

A full-grown black urchin may have a body or test nearly 4 inches in diameter, with spines 12 to 15 inches long. This is one of the comparatively few shore animals that are poisonous to the touch, and the effect of contact with one of the slender, hollow spines is said to be like that of a hornet sting, or may even be more serious for a child or an especially susceptible adult. Apparently the mucous coating of the spines bears the irritant or poison.

This urchin is extraordinary in the degree of its awareness of the surroundings. A hand extended over it will cause all the spines to swivel about on their mountings, pointing menacingly at the intruding object. If the hand is moved from side to side the spines swing about, following it. According to Professor Norman Millott of the University College of the West Indies, nerve receptors scattered widely over the body receive the message conveyed by a change in the intensity of light, responding most sharply to suddenly decreased light as a shadowy portent of danger. To this extent, then, the urchin may actually "see" moving objects passing nearby.

Linked in some mysterious way with one of the great rhythms of nature, this sea urchin spawns at the time of the full moon. The eggs and sperm are shed into the water once in each lunar month during the summer season, on the nights of strongest moonlight. Whatever the stimulus to which all the individuals of the species respond, it assures that prodigal and simultaneous release of reproductive cells that nature often demands for the perpetuation of a species.

Off some of the Keys, in shallow water, lives the so-called slate-pencil urchin, named for its short stout spines. This is an urchin of solitary habit, single individuals sheltering under or among the reef rocks near the low-tide level. It seems a sluggish creature of dull perceptions, unaware of the presence of an intruder, and making no effort to cling by means of its tube feet when it is picked up. It belongs to the only family of modern echinoderms that also existed in Paleozoic time; the recent members of the group show little change from the form of ancestors that lived hundreds of millions of years ago.

Another urchin with short and slender spines and color variations ranging from deep violet to green, rose, or white, sometimes occurs abundantly on sandy bottoms carpeted with turtle grass, camouflaging itself with bits of grass and shell and coral fragments held in its tube feet. Like many other urchins, it performs a geologic function. Nibbling away at shells and coral rock with its white teeth, it chips off fragments that are then passed through the grinding mill of its digestive tract; these organic fragments, trimmed, ground, and polished within the urchins, contribute to the sands of tropical beaches.

The Sting of Death

Of all the venomous marine organisms, perhaps the most lethal is the almost transparent blob of a jellyfish known as the sea wasp (opposite, top left). It has been called the deadliest creature alive, with a poisoning ability greater than that of any snake. Bathers stung by the sea wasp have died in the minutes it took them to stagger back to the beach. The sea wasp belongs to a marine phylum called Cnidaria, which includes jellyfish, hydroids, corals and sea anemones, all of which have stinging cells called nematocysts lining their tentacles.

There are a few hundred species of jellyfish (two are seen on this page), all of which are able to lie horizontally in the water and propel themselves with pulsating movements of their umbrella-like bodies (below). An often faster, although not always reliable, mode of locomotion is employed by the Portuguese man-of-war (opposite, below), a translucent hydroid. This creature, commonly mistaken for a jellyfish, moves with the help of an inflated, gas-filled bag which is raised out of the water ready to catch even the gentlest breeze.

The notorious sea wasp (above, left) is the scourge of Australia's beaches. In their search for food, such as bottom-dwelling shrimp, sea wasps move very close to shore and to bathers. Some sources estimate that as many as 50 bathers in Australian waters alone have died from the sea wasp's sting. Never deadly, though still dangerous, are the medusa jellyfish (above, right) and the Portuguese man-of-war (left), whose tentacles can deliver a nasty sting even after they are torn from their balloon-like bell.

Delicate and Dangerous

Hydroids, like the colonial hydroid above, are polyps that live cooperatively in colonies so lush and flowing that they resemble aquatic gardens of plants and flowers more than animals. Of the thousands of hydroid species, most are harmless to man. Some, however, are capable of inflicting stings that can cause intense pain and rashes that persist for several days. Among the most dangerous are the stinging, or fire, corals (opposite), which are not true corals but hydroids. The stinging corals are composed of two types of polyps, a large, wide-mouthed variety that catches tiny morsels of food for the colony and a small, mouthless type that is armed with stinging cells, called nematocysts, very much like those of a jellyfish. These polyps are concealed in calcified skeletons that many people are tempted to break off for a souvenir. The result of such impetuousness can be a searing, white-hot pain caused by the stinging cells, or a nasty wound inflicted by the skeleton's razor-sharp edges, or both.

Borgias of the Bottom

The sea cucumber (below) and the bristle worm (left), unlike many of the oceans' killers, are quite benign in appearance. Yet each possesses a toxin that can be deadly to other sea creatures. The venom of the bristle worm is carried in a poison sac located in a retractable proboscis at the front of the worm. When a worm is threatened it can extend this proboscis with great speed, strike the molester with the four fangs at its tip and inject a chemical that can cause paralysis. Furthermore, the worm's numerous needle-tipped bristles are sharp enough to cause painful wounds. The toxin of some sea cucumbers is located in tubules within the creature's body. If the sea cucumber senses danger it excretes the tubules into the water, where they swell and extend into long, sticky threads; these are capable of entangling and trapping a hapless victim. Some species of sea cucumbers produce a poison that is quite toxic. It can cause burning and inflammation on human skin and blindness, should it touch the eyes.

A Marauder and a Menace

Divers of the Pacific have long been aware of the descriptively named crown-of-thorns sea star shown below highly magnified. In the past it was commonly called a starfish although the animal is not a true fish. The sea star inflicts a mildly poisonous sting with the sturdy spines on its upper surface. In recent years, however, the prickly creature has threatened men in another way—by methodically destroying their environment. Attacking the living coral reefs of the South Pacific, enormous infestations of these sea stars have eaten away protective barrier reefs, and the islands themselves have begun to disintegrate. Scientists are at a loss to explain the sudden invasion. Another dangerous invertebrate is the sea urchin, *Toxopneustes roseus* (opposite), its venomous pedicellariae open and awaiting prey. As soon as a foreign object touches these tiny seizing organs they clamp shut and hold on stubbornly. Even if they are ripped from their shell, the pedicellariae may remain active and continue to bite for several hours.

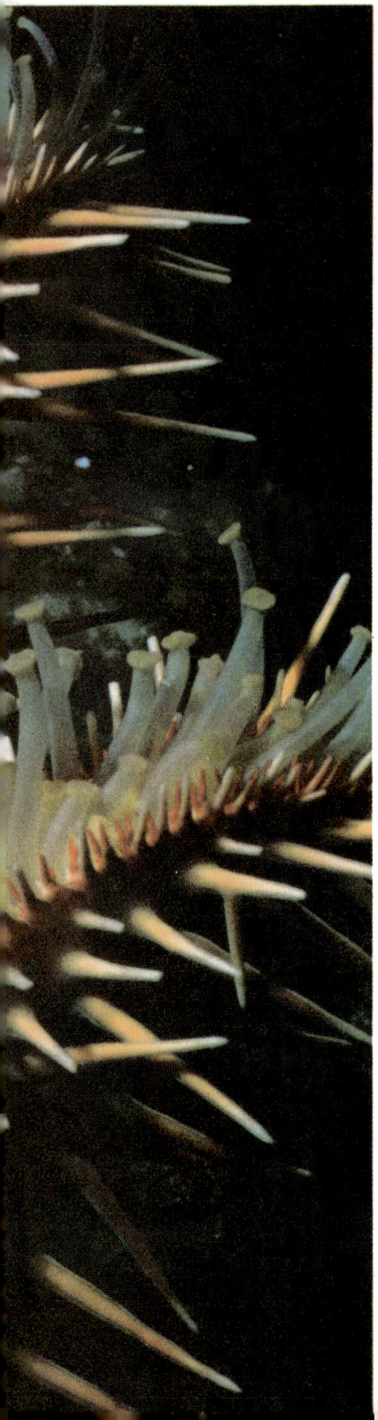

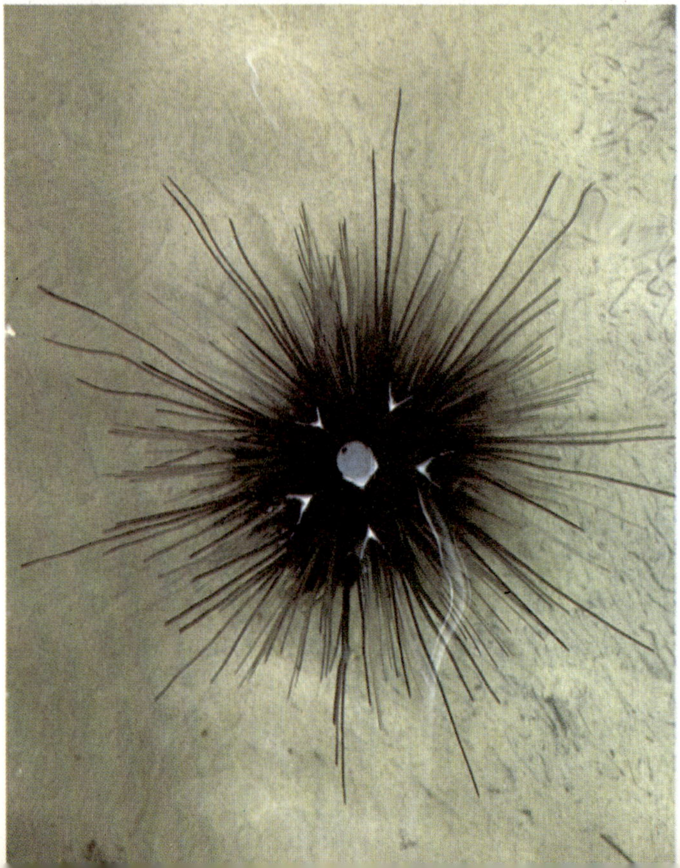

Poisonous Pin Cushion

The Greek name for the group of creatures that includes these sea urchins is an appropriate one: *Echinoderms*, or "prickle skins." It comes from the fact that urchins are covered with sharp spines that can be dramatically long—in the case of the *Diadema* (left and above) as much as a foot or more. An urchin's sting can inflict a painful wound that, in the most extreme cases, may lead to muscular paralysis and breathing difficulty. Some urchins' spines are extremely sharp and can easily penetrate deep into flesh; the tip, which is very brittle, breaks off and deposits a venom under the victim's skin. Divers must carefully avoid sea urchins, since even leather gloves and a wet suit are not complete protection against the creatures' deadly daggers.

Flowers That Sting

The beautiful, flowerlike sea anemones are distant cousins of the jellyfish. Unlike jellyfish the firmer, more muscular-bodied anemone spends most of its life firmly fixed in one spot, occasionally moving short distances and reattaching itself to a rock or coral. There are thousands of varieties of anemones (two are shown here), and they differ from one another in almost every way imaginable. One thing they all have in common is the ability to sting and paralyze their prey with specialized cells that line their tentacles. Anemones are tube-shaped animals, fixed to a firm surface at their bottom, with a mouth slit on top and an array of tentacles surrounding the mouth. They can devour enormous quantities of food, but when provender is scarce they can shrink their bodies to a fraction of their usual size without harm. An anemone will use its tentacles to seize and sting any creature that swims into reach, then pass the paralyzed catch into its mouth to be digested in the body.

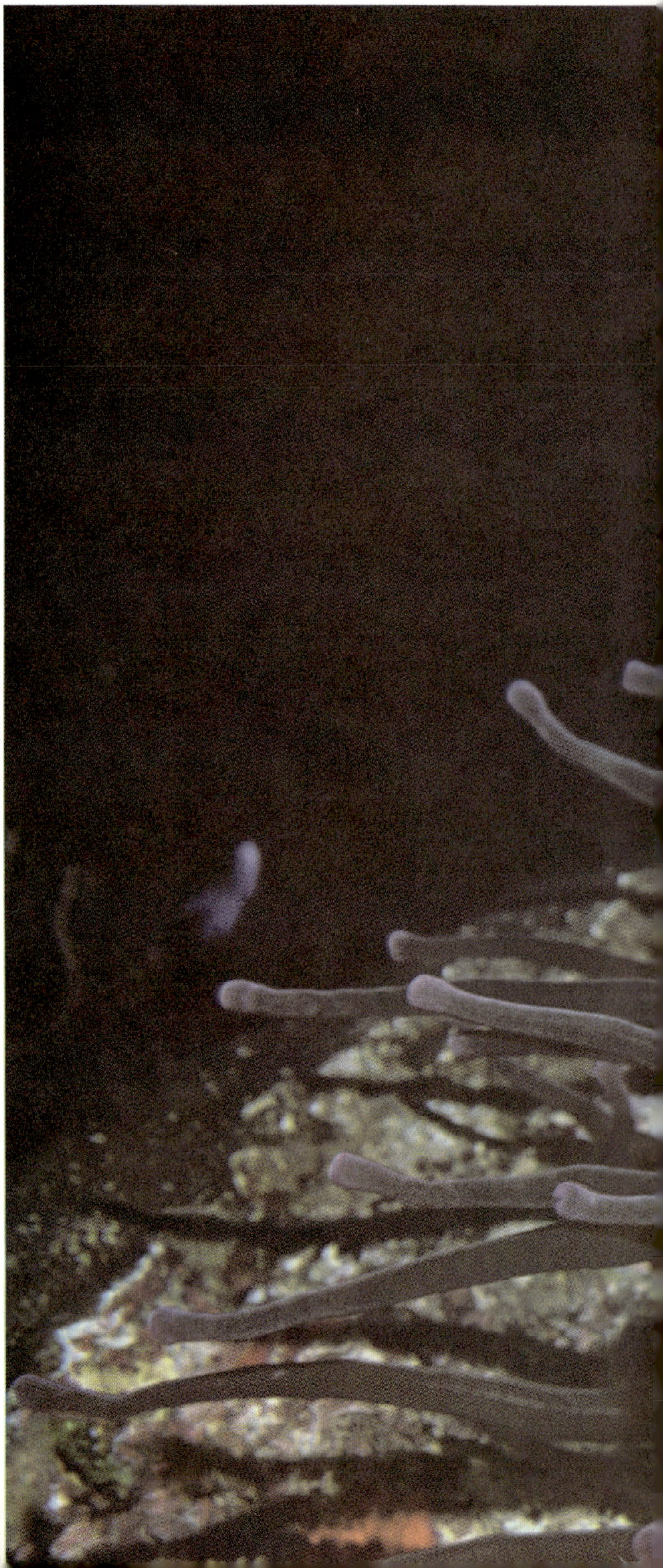

The anemone's tentacle is lined with sensitive stinging cells. When a fish—or diver—touches it, these cells, or nematocysts, are actuated to paralyze the hapless victim.

Anemone Anatomy

Sea anemones are one of the lowest and the loveliest looking forms of marine animal life. In the center of the animal, surrounded by swaying tentacles, is the mouth that leads to a stomach that makes up the anemone's entire body. In this cavity digestion occurs after the prey has been drawn into the anemone's mouth by the tentacles. These fingery appendages eventually disappear, along with the food, inside the cavity until digestion is completed (opposite and filmstrip at left). Sea anemones are carnivores and will eat almost any marine creature that gets within their reach. One exception is the brightly striped anemone fish, seen below. These creatures approach the anemone's tentacles gently and slowly. During this period of acclimatization they develop a slimy secretion that prevents the anemone's stinging nematocysts from discharging and allows the fish to weave in and out of the anemone's deadly arms unharmed.

An inevitable plot line in every old "B" movie about deep-sea divers was the scene where the hero accidently stepped into the yawning mouth of a giant clam and—snap!—he was trapped. This frightening possibility gave the creature its other name, "Killer Clam." In fact, however, there is not one authenticated case of a death resulting from a person being caught by a giant clam (left and above). There are records of narrow escapes, though, and pearl divers and others who regularly encounter the monsters give them a wide berth. They are the largest shelled mollusks, measuring as much as five feet across the lips and weighing 500 pounds or more. The luxuriant color of the species above results from a pigment in its fleshlike mantle.

Sea Snakes

On land the snake has adapted admirably to many environments, acquiring some impressive defenses, including stealth, speed in striking and, in many species, venom-armed fangs. But the serpents who discovered the best defense against the depredations of terrestrial predators are undoubtedly those whose ancestors decided to return to the sea from which they, like all animal life on the planet, had originally come. The result is the sea snake, another marine marvel of natural adaptation to environment.

When the snakes went back to the sea, they took with them two characteristics they had acquired during their eons-long terrestrial existence: air-breathing lungs and venomous fangs. In readapting to a watery way of life they also changed certain physiological equipment to enable them to move, feed and reproduce more efficiently in the thicker and more resistant aquatic environment. Some developed tails flattened vertically like an oar blade so that by wagging their posteriors from side to side they are able to propel themselves either forward or backward with equal speed and dexterity. Some also modified their scales, which do not overlap as extensively as do those of land snakes; in some species scales abut one another to form a continuous smooth covering, giving the seagoing serpent a more streamlined surface for slipping through the water.

But it is the retained characteristic of venomness that has made the sea snake one of the most dangerous marine animals. The sea snakes have not only kept the poisonous capability of some of their land-based cousins; they have also improved on it and made it universal among their family. Marine biologists estimate that some sea-snake venoms are from two to 50 times as virulent as that of the king cobra, and of the approximately 50 catalogued species of sea snakes, all are venomous. Despite this unanimity of poisonous potential, the sea snake remains a basically nonaggressive creature and bites only when it is provoked. Even then it does not always employ its stored noxious liquid. In fact it has been estimated that only 25 percent of all people bitten by sea snakes are poisoned. Nobody is quite sure why this should be so. Perhaps in such nonpoisonous encounters the venom glands were depleted from a recent attack. When the sea snake does use the venom, it is introduced into the victim by fangs set far forward in the snake's rather weak dentition. The principal function of the fangs appears to be to introduce venom that will at least partially paralyze prey, making it suitable for easy swallowing.

Humans bitten by sea snakes initially feel none of the violent pain that accompanies successful attacks by so many other venomous sea creatures. If the victim feels anything, it is no more than a pin prick, and because the ensuing symptoms develop very slowly, taking from 20 minutes to several hours, the snakebitten human often does not connect the bite with the progressive deterioration of his health. The mortality rate among those bitten and poisoned has been estimated as high as 25 percent. Fishermen are the most frequent victims, either from stepping on or handling a snake carelessly.

Sea snakes are themselves preyed upon only by nature's most wanton and omnivorous predators—man and shark—and occasionally by certain sea birds that dive on the snakes when they surface to breathe. All species of sea snakes have nostrils on top of their heads that permit them to respire by exposing only the smallest portion of their bodies. When they are submerged the respiratory opening is closed by a valve. The lung of the sea snake extends to its tail, enabling it to hold its breath and stay underwater for hours at a time. Other adaptations to marine existence include the ability of some species to bear their young alive in the open sea. Fetal sea snakes are coiled into tight balls, but, uncoiled, the newborn young can be quite large, nearly half as long as the mother (adult snakes range in length from three to nine feet) and are able to swim and forage from the moment they are born.

Probably the most fascinating—and puzzling—fact about sea snakes is that while differing species abound in all warm and temperate waters of the Indian and Pacific oceans, none has ever been found in the Atlantic Ocean or in the Mediterranean or Red seas. They have been seen around the Pacific entrance to the Panama Canal and on the eastern side of the Cape of Good Hope at the southern tip of Africa but never in the Atlantic. One lone species has adapted to fresh water and is found only in Lake Taal on the Philippine island of Luzon. Why they exist almost exclusively in Indo-Pacific waters nobody knows. Scientists have theorized that, being strictly warm-water creatures, they cannot survive or breed in the cold temperatures of the waters that separate the Atlantic and Pacific. Nor can they negotiate the Panama Canal because of the locks and freshwater lakes that form a part of that waterway.

Dangerous Curves

Sea snakes, one of the most widely distributed groups of reptiles in the world, are true snakes. They have juxtaposed, hexagonal scales covering their limbless bodies and immobile, lidless eyes covered by transparent scales. They move swiftly and easily through the water, with lateral undulating movements of their bodies (below), and get extra propulsion from their paddlelike tails. They need air to breathe but are able to remain submerged for hours at a time, due, it is thought, to their slow metabolism and single, enlarged lung. Without the rocks and shrubbery that land snakes rub against to clean themselves, sea snakes, like the one in the filmstrip at left, twist themselves into pretzel shapes and rub off debris and shedding skin with different parts of their own bodies. Sea snakes spend much of their time feeding. Some species eat only bottom-dwelling creatures such as eels and other small fish and have been known to dive to depths of 500 feet to search for them. Other snakes are exclusively surface feeders and lie motionlessly atop the water, resembling floating sticks, to which fish are attracted. Although the disposition of sea snakes ranges from docile to pugnacious, depending on the species, all are venomous and should be handled with care.

The sea snake's tongue, seen flicking out into the water from its small head (above) is slender and forked and serves to pick up scents in the water. It is covered with three layers of skin to protect it from abrasion and from exposure to the seawater. The head houses tiny and fragile teeth, plus a set of hollow fangs that are connected to the snake's venom glands. The fangs, which are easily broken or dislodged, are used to grasp, hold and chew prey rather than strike or stab it.

Sea Monsters

The sea is calm and the night quiet. Leaden clouds obscure the moon but do not prevent its filtered brilliance from illuminating the ocean with a somber, low-intensity light that makes the horizon seem very close. The sailor on watch on the cargo ship is bored with staring into the half-darkness and finds himself almost dozing on his feet. Suddenly off the starboard bow a serpentine figure appears, undulating segments standing out clearly even in the poor light as the animal slithers through the water. Looking for the creature's head, the sailor is not sure but thinks he can see a long, rearing neck and a small head with beady eyes. Counting the glistening segments as they are exposed, the lookout discerns at least a dozen, each having a minimum length of 10 feet. That adds up to a monstrous creature at least 120 feet long! The sailor excitedly sounds the alarm, and one more sea-monster sighting goes slithering into the record books.

Encounters such as this have taken place thousands of times since men first took to the sea in ships, and they continue into our present, coldly scientific age. Inasmuch as the sea is already filled with so many real and identifiable dangers, it would seem unnecessary for mankind to invent others of even more awesome proportions. But there are only three ways of interpreting the mystery of sea monsters: explain them away as mistaken identification of known natural phenomena; accept that there are creatures of extraordinary sizes and shapes living in the sea that science has not yet identified; or attribute the entire matter to the limitless imagination of man. If the third explanation prevails, then it must follow that the sea and the creatures that dwell therein, both those that are and those that might be, have provided man with the stuff of dreams and nightmares for at least 3,000 years.

Sea monsters abound in the mythology of the Chinese, Indians, Egyptians, Babylonians and other ancient peoples, but the earliest detailed description of the creatures was written by the Greek poet Homer about 800 B.C. (see page 123). In Book XII of the *Odyssey* Homer describes two sea monsters, Scylla and Charybdis. The model for Charybdis was evidently a whirlpool. But for the prototype of the six-headed, 12-footed Scylla, Homer may only have embroidered on what he had heard about the giant squid—which has 10 tentacles, or arms, instead of 12—or the eight-tentacled octopus, in which case his foot count is even more in error.

The giant squid is certainly the origin of Scandinavia's mighty *kraken*, represented repeatedly in words and drawings from the 16th century on as attacking and sinking oceangoing ships with its great and powerful tentacles. Modern experts believe it quite possible that huge specimens of the giant cephalopod may have at times attacked and even sunk ships at sea. In this case, myth and fact have become so mixed that 20th-century Norwegians use the word *kraken* interchangeably to mean both "sea monster" and "giant squid." Not so easily pinned down is the real-life prototype of Grendel, the villain of the earliest epic poem in Anglo-Saxon literature, *Beowulf*. Grendel, described as half human and half sea monster, had the habit of breaking into the palace of the Danish king every night and carrying away his men, until the noble warrior Beowulf fought and wounded him mortally, after which Grendel went to a far-off sea to die.

Marine monsters crowd the legends and literature of all lands and all ages, from the Biblical leviathan, described in Isaiah XXVII as a "twisting serpent" and "a dragon that is in the sea," to the present, a time when man almost nonchalantly accepts the scientific realities of the splitting of the atom and space travel and yet revels in the mystery of the Loch Ness monster. "Nessie," who first achieved international fame in 1933, is probably the best-known monster of all time, having been repeatedly sighted by people of excellent repute, such as clergymen, schoolteachers and scientists. Unfortunately, very few of the Loch Ness sighters were carrying cameras at the time, although some blurred photographs do exist. New but inconclusive photographs continue to turn up.

The great majority of sea monsters reported over the years are serpentine in shape and have a minimum length of 20 feet; the sea snake, which is surely the most logical prototype of a sea serpent, grows no longer than half that

This 1934 photograph still remains the strongest evidence for the existence of the Loch Ness monster.

length. Yet not all the monsters have been ugly or repulsive: The mermaidlike sirens of Homeric mythology who enticed seamen to their deaths with sweet song had all the charms of beautiful females.

All kinds of rationalizations have been put forward to explain sea-monster phenomena. One favorite theory holds that a dozen dolphins leaping in a line could be mistaken for a sea serpent. The giant squid with its 30-foot-long tentacles is an obvious candidate for mistaken identity, as is the oarfish, an elongated creature that grows to 20 feet and swims at surface level with undulating movements. The manatee and the dugong, sluggish warm-water sea cows that have shortened foreflippers and prominent bosoms, are undoubtedly prototypes of the mermaid. Distant glimpses, blurred by grog and long womanless days and nights at sea, could easily have given rise to such a wishful legend. As for the more unpleasant varieties of monsters, there are many other explanations. In 1959 a six-foot larval eel was taken off the coast of Africa at a depth of 1,000 feet. Eel larvae are normally only a few

A 16th-century artist's imagination supplied details for the woodcut (left) that purports to show a whale's angry reaction to sailors who mistook it for an island. Closer to reality is the sketch (below) of a sea serpent that was cast ashore at Hungary Bay, Bermuda, in 1860.

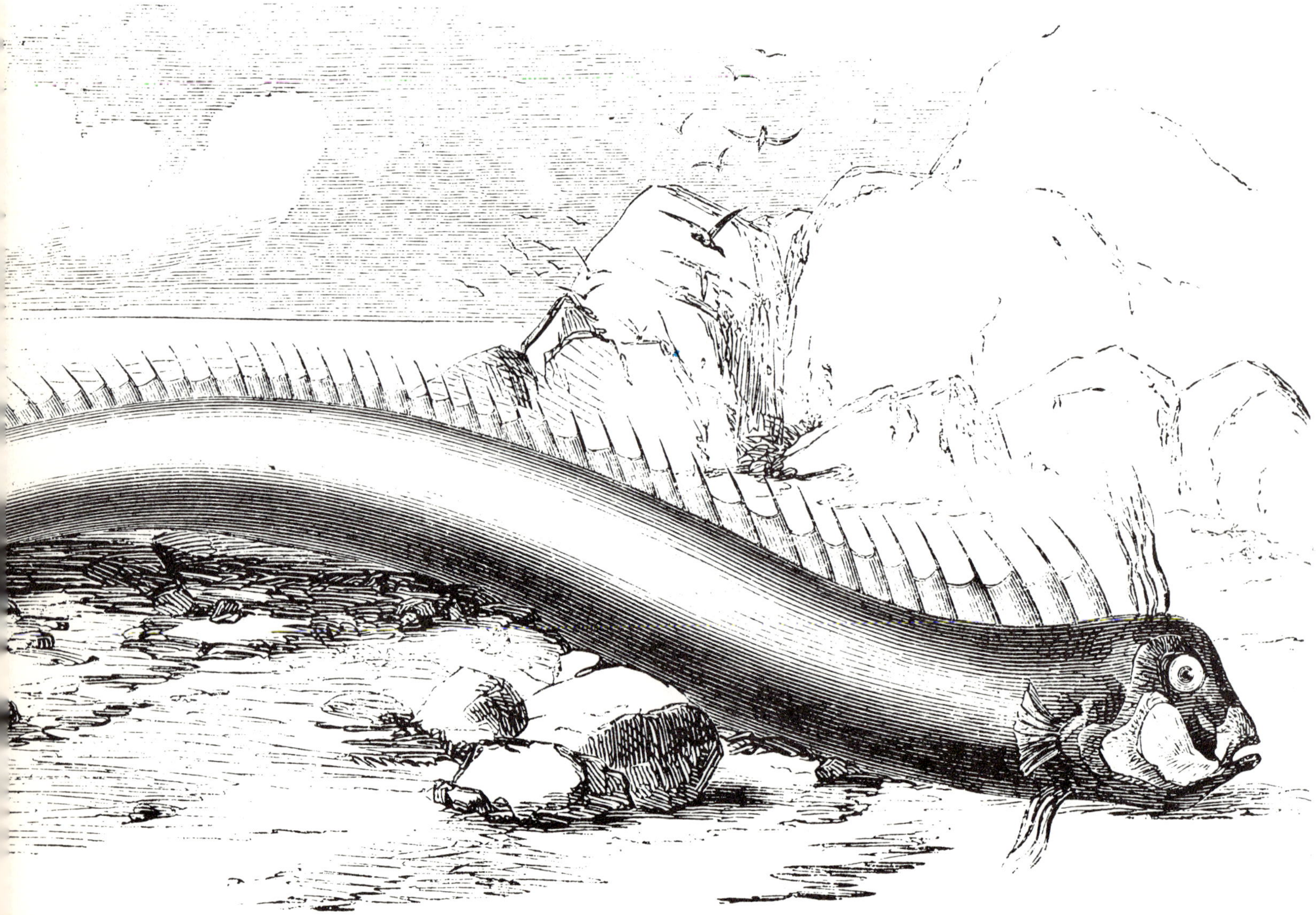

The confused reports by survivors of a wreck off Boston in 1819 gave rise to this lithograph.

inches long, and at that time some marine zoologists estimated that an adult eel giving birth to a six-foot larva must be at least 60 to 70 feet long, far bigger than any of the species ever measured. This theory is no longer taken seriously, and many believe that the Great Sea Serpent may be nothing more than a gigantic eel that lives in the deepest trenches and surfaces only on rare occasions.

A notion with more romantic appeal is that sea monsters do exist. Certain true believers contend that the monsters are holdovers from earlier times now thought to be extinct, such as the long-necked plesiosaur, which roamed the waters of the world 70 million years ago and whose fossil remains look startlingly like the images projected by most sea-monster reports. If the coelacanth—a 300-million-year-old fish thought to be extinct for millions of years until the spectacular discovery of a living specimen in 1938—can still roam the ocean, why not a plesiosaur? Or some similar monster that left no fossil remains but still lives in the depths, rising only occasionally to scare the wits out of a lonely sailor on lookout duty?

Fire in the Galley Stove

by William Outerson

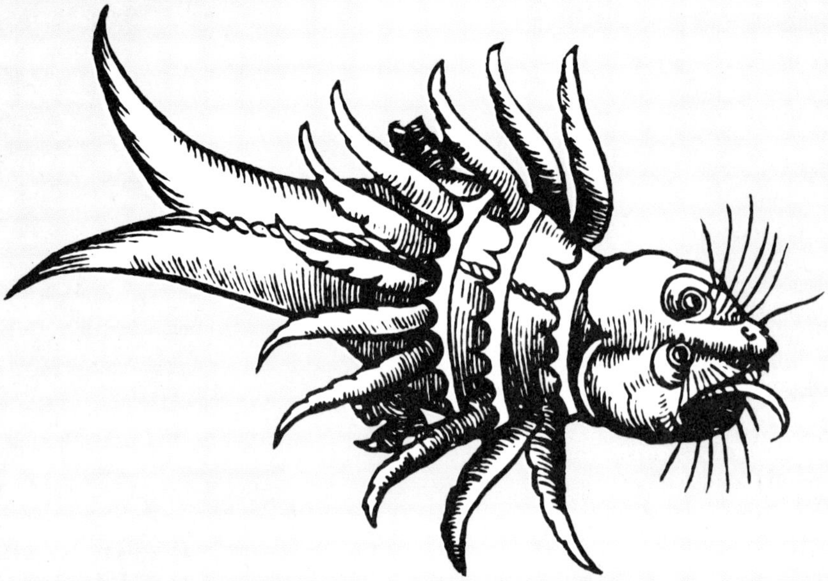

A little more than 100 years ago a ship, the Marie Celeste, *was sighted sailing aimlessly near the Azores. When she was boarded, a mystery, still unsolved, was revealed. The cargo hold, the galley and the living quarters were found to be in order; the last entry in the log, written on November 25, 1872, hinted of no trouble; but there was no sign of captain or crew. The hatches were open, the compass smashed, the helm loose. What happened? Perhaps we will never know. Several theories have been offered to explain the mystery, some more plausible than others but none more exciting than short-story writer William Outerson presented in "Fire in the Galley Stove." Outerson calls his ship the* Unicorn, *but the story's end clearly indicates that the author patterned his fictional account after the real tale of the* Marie Celeste.

The first hint that the Unicorn's *crew has of impending disaster is a gentle bump on the ship's bottom, followed by a gigantic tidal wave that washes over the ship. Suddenly the wheel is jammed by something on the rudder.*

The skipper and the mate still waited at the taffrail for a sight of the things from the deep, and the long inaction had begun to affect their nerves.

"If we could only see them, and find out what they are," muttered the captain, "we might be able to decide on some plan of action. But how can we fight against invisible things of unknown nature!" He paced back and forth along a short path between the taffrail and the standard binnacle, frowning impatiently, clenching and opening his hands nervously.

Mister Mergam had glanced forward at the sound of the cook's gong, and he watched the men as they came out of the forecastle and went to the galley door to await their turn for coffee. The first man in line received his coffee and started for the fore hatch, where he intended to sit while drinking it. He did not see the long slender tentacle that quirted over the rail above his head and waved here and there seeking what it might find.

It found old Charlie as he reached the fore hatch, concealed from his watchmates by the corner of the forward house, wrapped itself around his neck with a strangling hold that prevented him from uttering a sound, and dragged him violently over the rail.

The next man, following with his coffee, saw Charlie at the rail, striking madly at the tentacle with his hook-pot, and a startled yell attracted the attenion of the others. They spun around and saw old Charlie going over the side in a headlong dive with his waving hook-pot, but were too late to notice the deadly tentacle around his neck. They rushed to the rail and stared down at the dull water, but the man who had seen the tentacle held back. He knew the sort of beast it belonged to.

Men may sail the seas for a lifetime and seldom, if ever, come in contact with the nightmare monsters that inhabit the caves and cliffs of the ocean floor. Gazing down at the slightly muddy water, the men of the *Unicorn* saw a squirming mass of interwoven tentacles resembling enormous snakes, immensely thick and long and tapering at their free ends to the size of a man's thumb. It was a foul

sight, an obscene growth from the dark places of the world, where incessant hunger is the driving force. At one place, down near the bulge of the hull, appeared a staring gorgon face with great lidless eyes and a huge parrot beak that moved slightly, opening and shutting as though it had just crunched and swallowed a meal of warm flesh. In its neighborhood the water was stained a reddish hue, possibly with blood from the veins of old Charlie. There were many of those deep-sea devils under the ship, ravenously hungry and now aware that there was food on her decks in the form of puny bodies that could be had for the taking.

Suddenly the men of the watch saw the air above the rail alive with tentacles. They swayed uncertainly for a second or two in order to feel the position of their prey, then lashed out with swift aim at the horrified men. Whipping round them, they tightened their hold to a vise-like grip that no human strength could break, though a sharp knife could slice them in two if properly used. The men were panic-stricken and struck wildly with sheath knives and hook-pots, but failed in their excitement to cut themselves off and went over the rail screaming. The boatswain, carpenter, and sailmaker jumped up from the main hatch and rushed across the deck to rescue the few survivors of the watch, but half a dozen tentacles seized them and jerked them over the side.

When the first tentacle came over the rail and fastened itself on Charlie, the steward was ambling forward to the galley for the cabin coffee. On seeing the man dragged violently over the rail the steward stopped and stared in amazement, trying to imagine what had happened to the sailor and thinking that perhaps he had become suddenly insane. The reeling gait of old Charlie, however, his struggles and the manner in which he went over the rail, convinced the steward that something had hold of him. His smooth-shaven face, round and placid, became puckered with anxiety and he stared in growing consternation at the struggle that developed between the men of the watch and the tapering tentacles that whipped over the rail in dozens. While he stood watching this primitive contest, a tentacle flung itself around his waist and dragged him down before his whimper could rise to a scream of terror.

The cook with the flaming hair came out of the galley with a carving knife and tried to run aft to the poop, but was caught. He slashed off the tentacle but was seized by others and dragged over, the severed tentacle clinging around his body. The men of the starboard watch tumbled out with drawn knives in ready hands. They had to divide forces to protect themselves on both sides, as the tentacles were now swaying above each rail from forecastle to poop. Though they fought with fury and some skill they had small chance to win against such desperate odds. Some of them jumped into the rigging to get out of reach by climbing aloft, but the men who tried that exposed themselves to the beasts lurking below and were snatched away immediately. There were too many tentacles to be cut, and even when they were slashed clean through they continued to cling around a man's body. They had suction cups on their under sides and rings of sharp claws within these.

"There's the answer," said the mate to the skipper when the battle began after the death of old Charlie. "The things sticking to the bottom are giant octopuses. They're the biggest things in the sea, except for the whales, and only the sperm whale can tackle them. He feeds on them, and sometimes they feed on him, if they can hold him down till he drowns. I'll get a knife and give the men a hand."

"Better do that than stand here telling me things I already know," the skipper retorted sharply. "There's men dying forward there."

The mate hurried to the companionway. He would go to his room for a hunting knife he kept there—a beautiful weapon hitherto useless, with an eight-inch blade as sharp as a razor. The octopus which had folded itself over the stern and jammed the rudder, aware that its companions were obtaining food from the top of this rocklike mass they were clinging to, flung two tentacles over the taffrail and waved one of them in Mister Mergam's direction.

"Look out, sir!" The man at the wheel screamed a warning.

Mister Mergam was just about to descend the companionway when he heard this cry. He threw a swift glance over his shoulder, saw the thing flicking toward him, and tried to jump down the companionway. He was too late. The tentacle wrapped itself around his chest and tightened. He strained against it, uttering a faint grunt, and braced himself with hands and feet against the hatch.

"Bring a knife, sir, and cut me loose," he implored the captain. The latter stared at him in horror and rushed away for a knife, going down the poop ladder to the door leading to the cabin from the main deck.

Another tentacle found the man at the wheel and caught him around the waist, binding one arm to his side but leaving the other free. It was the rule aboard the *Unicorn* that no seaman should wear a knife while standing his trick at the wheel, therefore Thomson carried none. He knew that human strength could not prevail against the power of these tentacles, though they could be cut, and he waited for the return of the skipper with the knife. Meantime, he made a sudden jerk and dragged the tentacle a couple of feet toward him, wrapped two turns of it around a spoke of the wheel, and held it fast there. It required desperate strength to do that with one hand, and he succeeded only because he was an exceptionally powerful man. Now the octopus could not drag him over the side without breaking the spoke, which was teakwood and very tough.

The mate had nothing but his hands, and these could not serve him. A sharp ax hung on the bulkhead a few steps below him in the companionway, and he made supreme efforts to go down there to secure this weapon. He was unsuccessful, for the octopus refused to slacken up and tightened its grip till the mate groaned with the pain of it.

Though the skipper had not been gone more than a few minutes, Mister Mergam thought he would never come back and cried in a gasping voice for him to hurry. Captain Garton shouted that he could not find the knife in the mate's cabin and was bringing the ax from the bulkhead. He was coming right up.

"For God's sake, hurry!" the mate entreated. "The brute's crushing me."

The skipper wrenched the ax out of the slings and staggered up the companionway to cut Mister Mergam free, but as he reached him the mate was dragged violently away from the hatch. Captain Garton followed in urgent pursuit. Dashing out on deck, he made a swift step toward the unfortunate mate and swung the ax for a severing stroke, but before the blade fell Mister Mergam was whipped with a crash against the taffrail and went down over the side.

The man at the wheel found it difficult to hold against the pull of the octopus, even with a double turn of the tentacle around the spoke. He was gasping and purple in the face, and the harder he strove against it the tighter the tentacle was drawn. He was rapidly becoming exhausted.

After peering over the side for a few precious seconds to see what had become of his lost mate, the skipper drew back from the rail horrified and trembling. He was not a strong man. Turning toward the wheel, he noted the perilous plight of the man there, and stumbled across the deck intending to sever the tentacle where it was wrapped around the spoke. In his condition of quaking repulsion he could hardly lift the ax and stood for seconds trying to swing it above his head.

The octopus jamming the rudder eased its pressure down there, and the wheel spun around under the pull of the tentacle, which slipped off the spoke. Thomson was hurtled across the poop and over the side, crashing against the skipper and knocking him down. The ax fell from Captain Garton's hands, and he rose staggering to pick it up. As he seized it he saw another tentacle whipping over the rail toward him, and in a surge of blind fury he swung the ax, which left his hands and went flashing into the sea. He swooned when the tentacle gripped him, and the octopus drew him down.

Cowering on the forecastle head, the man on lookout saw the last of the crew go down to feed the octopuses, and his mind roved in every direction searching for a means of saving his own life. Up to the present no tentacles had come up over the head rail, and he stood absolutely still, hoping that they would not find him.

But in this he was disappointed. One of them came up and waved about, drawing nearer every second. Out of his mind with terror, the lookout sprang to the rail and saw in the water below the appalling face of an octopus. Taking his knife by the blade, he threw it with miraculous aim and saw it sink out of sight in the eye of the beast, which went into a tremendous flurry. Looking aft, the man saw that there were few tentacles now waving over the main deck, and he crept down the ladder to look for a knife. Stealing along the port side, he searched eagerly but could not find one, returned along the starboard side, and met the same result. All the men had gone down fighting with the knives and the hook-pots in their hands. Reaching the fore hatch, he decided to enter the forecastle and shut the door. The ports were already closed. But he was just a moment too late. They got him.

A little while later a pod of sperm whales came up to blow not far from the *Unicorn*; and the octopuses, feeling the near presence of their deadly enemies, went away from there and returned to the deep places.

The ship *Merivale*, heading eastward some days out of New York, sighted a ship with all sail set. She was observed to behave in an erratic manner and appeared to be abandoned, since there was nobody at the wheel or about the decks. In the gentle breeze that was blowing shortly after sunrise the strange vessel bore away to the west, came up in the wind with all her canvas flapping, paid off slowly, and bore away again, repeating this endlessly. The skipper and the second mate of the *Merivale* watched her queer behavior from the poop, and, as no answer was made to their signals, a boat was sent off to the stranger to investigate.

The boat pulled alongside the *Unicorn*, and the second mate was boosted to the rail. They hove up the boat's painter, which he made fast, and scrambled up beside him. Except for some stains of coffee on the foredeck, which had not completely dried, the decks were clear and shipshape. In the cabin the second mate noted that the table was set for coffee, but the dishes had not been used. He scratched his head in complete bewilderment. All the boats were in the chocks, their covers untouched, and there was no sign of disease or mutiny. As he stood pondering the mysterious situation, one of his men came aft and halted in front of him.

"They ain't been gone very long, sir," he reported. "The fire's still fresh in the galley stove."

ODYSSEY

by Homer

The Odyssey, *Homer's epic, is a tale replete with gods and goddesses, heroes and cowards, monsters and loathsome creatures. At the center of the tale is Odysseus, King of Ithaca and Greek hero of the Trojan War. His ten-year postwar journey, with its dangers, terrors and tragedies, is described in a story that retains its fascination more than 2,000 years after its creation.*

In the following excerpt the goddess Circe, having warned Odysseus of the danger of the Sirens, tells him of other perils that lie in his path, and the hero makes the harrowing trip between Scylla and Charybdis.

"In the other direction lie two rocks, the higher of which rears its sharp peak up to the very sky and is capped by black clouds that never stream away nor leave clear weather round the top, even in summer or at harvest-time. . . . It is the home of Scylla, the creature with the dreadful bark. It is true that her yelp is no louder than a new-born pup's, but she is a horrible monster nevertheless, and one whom nobody could look at with delight, not even a god if he passed that way. She has twelve feet, all dangling in the air, and six long necks, each ending in a grisly head with triple rows of teeth, set thick and close, and darkly menacing death. Up to her middle she is sunk in the depths of the cave, but her heads protrude from the fearful abyss, and thus she fishes from her own abode, scouting around the rock for any dolphin or swordfish she may catch, or any of the larger monsters which in their thousands find their living in the roaring seas. No crew can boast that they ever sailed their ship past Scylla without loss, since from every passing vessel she snatches a man with each of her heads and so bears off her prey.

"The other of the two rocks is lower, as you, Odysseus, will see, and the distance between them is no more than a bowshot. A great fig-tree with luxuriant foliage grows upon the crag, and it is below this that dread Charybdis sucks the dark waters down. Three times a day she spews them up, and three times she swallows them down once more in her horrible way. Heaven keep you from the spot when she is at her work, for not even the Earthshaker could save you from disaster. No: you must hug Scylla's rock and with all speed drive your ship through, since it is far better that you should have to mourn the loss of six of your company than that of your whole crew." . . .

I was much perturbed in spirit and before long took my men into my confidence. "My friends," I said, "it is not right that only one or two of us should know the prophecies that Circe, in her divine wisdom, has made to me, and I am going to pass them on to you, so that we may all be forewarned, whether we die or escape the worst and save our lives. Her first warning concerned the mysterious Sirens. We must beware of their song and give their flowery meadow a wide berth. I alone, she suggested, might listen to their voices; but you must bind me hard and fast, so that I cannot stir from the spot where you will stand me, by the step of the mast, with the rope's ends lashed round the mast itself. And if I beg you to release me, you must tighten and add to my bonds."

I thus explained every detail to my men. In the meantime our good ship, with that perfect wind to drive her, fast approached the Sirens' Isle. But now the breeze dropped, some power lulled the waves, and a breathless calm set in. Rising from their seats my men drew in the sail and threw it into the hold, then sat down at the oars and churned the water white with their blades of polished pine. Meanwhile I took a large round of wax, cut it up small with my sword, and kneaded the pieces with all the strength of my fingers. The wax soon yielded to my vigorous treatment and grew warm, for I had the rays of my Lord the Sun to help me. I took each of my men in turn and plugged their ears with it. They then made me a prisoner on my ship by binding me hand and foot, standing me up by the step of the mast and tying the rope's ends to the mast itself. This done, they sat down once more and struck the grey water with their oars.

We made good progress and had just come within call of the shore when the Sirens became aware that a ship was swiftly bearing down upon them, and broke into their liquid song. . . .

The lovely voices came to me across the water, and my heart was filled with such a longing to listen that with nod and frown I signed to my men to set me free. But they swung forward to their oars and rowed ahead, while Perimedes and Eurylochus jumped up, tightened my bonds and added more. However, when they had rowed past the Sirens and we could no longer hear their voices and the burden of their song, my good companions were quick to clear their ears of the wax I had used to stop them, and to free me from my shackles.

We had no sooner put this island behind us than I saw a cloud of smoke ahead and a raging surf, the roar of which I could already hear. My men were so terrified that the oars all dropped from their grasp and fell with a splash in the wash of the ship; while the ship herself, now that the hands that had pulled the long blades were idle, was brought to a standstill. I made a tour of the vessel, and with a soothing word for each man I tried to put heart into my company. . . .

Thus we sailed up the straits, groaning in terror, for on the one side we had Scylla, while on the other the mysterious Charybdis sucked down the salt sea water in her dreadful way. When she vomited it up, she was stirred to her depths and seethed over like a cauldron on a blazing fire; and the spray she flung on high rained down on the tops of the crags at either side. But when she swallowed the salt water down, the whole interior of her vortex was exposed, the rocks re-echoed to her fearful roar, and the dark sands of the sea bottom came into view.

My men turned pale with fear; and now, while all eyes were fixed on Charybdis and the quarter from which we looked for disaster, Scylla snatched out of my boat the six ablest hands I had on board. I swung round, to glance at the ship and run my eye over the crew, just in time to see the arms and legs of her victims dangled high in the air above my head. "Odysseus!" they called out to me in their agony. But it was the last time they used my name. For like an angler on a jutting point, who with a long rod casts his ox-horn lure into the sea as bait for the little fish below, gets a bite, and whips his struggling prize to land, Scylla had whisked my comrades up and swept them struggling to the rocks, where she devoured them at her own door, shrieking and stretching out their hands to me in their last desperate throes. In all I have gone through as I made my way across the seas, I have never had to witness a more pitiable sight than that.

Tidal pools in a wildlife preserve in Southern California

Credits

Cover—Ron Taylor from Ardea Photographics. 1—Ben Cropp. 5—David Doubilet. 6—(left) H. Gruhl from Photo Aquatics, (top, right) David Doubilet, (bottom right) David Doubilet. 6–7—(center) David Doubilet. 7—(top, right) Eliot Elisofon, Time, Inc., (bottom) Neville Coleman from Sea Library. 9—Paul Chesley. 17—Ron Taylor from Ardea Photographics. 18–19—Peter Lake from Sea Library. 19—Ron and Valerie Taylor. 22–23—Valerie Taylor from Ardea Photographics. 24—Elgin Ciampi. 25—(left, top) Andrew A. Gifford from National Audubon Society Collection/Photo Researchers, Inc., (center, right) David Doubilet, (bottom, left) Ron and Valerie Taylor. 26–27—Valerie Taylor from Ardea Photographics. 27—(top, right) Peter Lake, (bottom, right) David Doubilet from Sea Library. 28—David Doubilet. 29—(left) David Doubilet, (right, top to bottom) Andrew A. Gifford from National Audubon Society Collection/Photo Researchers, Inc. 34—B. Evans from Sea Library. 35—J. Flannery from Bruce Coleman, Inc. 36—Ben Cropp. 37—David Doubilet. 39—David Doubilet. 40—(top) J. & C. Church from Sea Library, (bottom) Joel Sill from Sea Library. 41—Valerie Taylor from Ardea Photographics. 42—Ben Cropp. 43—John S. Flannery from Bruce Coleman, Inc. 44—(top) David Doubilet, (bottom) Dick Hoogerwerf from Sea Library. 45—(top)B. Evans from Sea Library, (bottom) C. Roessler from Sea Library. 47—Jen and Des Bartlett from Bruce Coleman, Inc. 48—(top) B. Evans from Sea Library, (center) Tom McHugh from Photo Researchers, Inc., (bottom) David Doubilet. 49—Tom McHugh for Steinhart Aquarium/Photo Researchers, Inc. 51—P. Morris from Ardea Photographics. 52–53—Tom McHugh for Steinhart Aquarium/Sea Library. 53—(center) Don Ollis, courtesy Dr. Bruce Halstead/World Life Research Institute, (bottom) Tony Mann. 55—S. Keiser from Sea Library. 56–57—Valerie Taylor from Ardea Photographics. 57—David Doubilet. 58—C. Roessler from Sea Library. 59—(top) Steinhart Aquarium from Sea Library, (bottom) B. Campoli from Sea Library. 60—(top) Lou Barr from Sea Library, (bottom) C. Roessler from Sea Library. 61—(top) Walter A. Starck II from Sea Library, (bottom) S. Keiser from Sea Library. 63—David Doubilet. 64—Valerie Taylor from Ardea Photographics. 65—(top) B. Evans from Sea Library, (bottom) C. Roessler from Sea Library. 66, 67—C. Roessler from Sea Library. 68—(top) David Doubilet, (bottom) C. Roessler from Sea Library. 69—David Doubilet. 70, 71—C. Roessler from Sea Library. 73—C. Roessler from Sea Library. 74, 75—W. van Heukelem. 81—(top) Walter Starck II from Sea Library, (bottom) David Doubilet. 82—(top) Gini Kellogg from Sea Library. 82–83—S. Keiser from Sea Library. 83—(top) Durrant Kellogg from Sea Library, (bottom) Mick Church from Sea Library. 85—B. Evans from Sea Library. 86—Neville Coleman from Sea Library. 87—(top) Timothy Turnbull, (bottom) C. Roessler from Sea Library. 88–89—Tony Mann. 94—(top) Walter Starck II from Sea Library, (bottom) S. Keiser from Sea Library. 95—(top, left) Neville Coleman from Sea Library, (top, right) Al Giddings from Sea Library, (bottom) Mick Church from Sea Library. 96—C. Roessler from Sea Library. 97—B. Evans from Sea Library. 98—C. Roessler from Sea Library. 99—H. Genthe from Sea Library. 100–101—David Doubilet. 101—Don Webber, courtesy Dr. Bruce Halstead/World Life Research Institute. 102—(top) C. Roessler from Sea Library, (bottom) Anthony Healy, courtesy Dr. Bruce Halstead/World Life Research Institute. 103—Joel Sill from Sea Library. 104, 105—C. Roessler from Sea Library. 106—S. Keiser from Sea Library. 107—John Boland from Sea Library. 108–109—David Doubilet. 109—C. Roessler from Sea Library. 111–S. Keiser from Sea Library. 112–C. Roessler from Sea Library. 113–Gini Kellogg from Sea Library. 115–Associated Press. 125–L. Dunmire from Sea Library. 128–Ben Cropp.

Photographs on endpapers are used courtesy of Time-Life Picture Agency and Russ Kinne and Stephen Dalton of Photo Researchers, Inc.

Film sequences on pages 8, 13, 42–43, 106 and 112 are from "Survival in the Sea," "Should Oceans Meet" and "Octopus," programs in the Time-Life Televison series *Wild, Wild World of Animals*.

ILLUSTRATIONS on pages 10–11, 14 and 23 are by Howard Koslow; the painting on page 24 is by Richard Ellis, the illustration on page 37 is by Jack Long; those on pages 20–21, 54, 90–93 are by André Durenceau; those on pages 30–33, 77–80 are by Michael Berenstain. The illustration on page 123 is by Martin and Alice Provensen; the illustration on page 15 is by Norman Weaver; the illustrations on pages 114 and 116 are used courtesy of the New York Public Library; and those on pages 117, 118, 119 and 121 are used courtesy of the Bettmann Archive, Inc.

Bibliography

NOTE: Asterisk at the left means that a paperback volume is also available.

*Balridge, H. David, *Shark Attack*. Berkley Publishing Company, 1974.

Bates, Marston, *The Forest and the Sea*. Random House, 1960.

Beebe, William, and Tee-Van, John, *Field Study of the Shore Fishes of Bermuda and the West Indies*. Dover Publications, 1933.

Bucherl, W., and Buckley, E., *Venomous Animals and Their Venom*. Vol. II—*Venomous Vertebrates*. Academic Press, 1971.

Budker, Paul, *The Life of Sharks*. Columbia University Press, 1971.

Burton, Maurice, *The Elusive Monster: An Analysis of the Evidence from Loch Ness*. Rupert Hart-Davis, 1961.

Caras, Roger, *Venomous Animals of the World*. Westover, 1973.

*Carson, Rachel, *The Edge of the Sea*. Houghton Mifflin, 1955.

*———, *Under the Sea Wind*. Oxford University Press, 1952.

Clare, Patricia, *The Struggle for the Great Barrier Reef*. Walker and Company, 1972.

Cook, Joseph, and Wisner, William, *The Phantom World of the Squid and Octopus*. Dodd, Mead, 1965.

*Cousteau, Jacques, *The Living Sea*. Harper & Row, 1963.

*———, *The Silent World*. Harper & Row, 1953.

Cromie, William J., *The Living World of the Sea*. Prentice-Hall Inc., 1966.

Dunson, William A., ed., *The Biology of Sea Snakes*. University Park Press, 1975.

Engel, Leonard, *The Sea*. Time-Life Books, 1972.

Gilbert, Perry W., ed., *Sharks and Survival*. D.C. Heath and Company, 1963.

Gilbert, Perry W.; Matthewson, Robert F.; and Rall, David P., eds., *Sharks, Skates and Rays*. Johns Hopkins Press, 1967.

Grzimek, Bernhard, *Grzimek's Animal Life Encyclopedia*. Fishes IV. Van Nostrand Reinhold, 1973. Fishes II and Amphibians. Van Nostrand Reinhold, 1974.

Halstead, Bruce W., *Dangerous Marine Animals*. Cornell Maritime Press, 1959.

———, *Poisonous and Venomous Marine Animals of the World*. Darwin Press, 1974.

Hardy, Alister, *The Open Sea: Its Natural History*. Houghton Mifflin, 1965.

*Helm, Thomas, *Shark! Unpredictable Killer of the Sea*. The Macmillan Company, 1963.

Heuvelmans, Bernard, *In the Wake of the Sea Serpents*. Hill and Wang, 1968.

*Heyerdahl, Thor, *Kon Tiki*. Rand McNally and Company, 1950.

Lane, Frank, *Kingdom of the Octopus*. Sheridan House, 1960.

Lucas, Joseph, and Critch, Pamela, *Life in the Oceans*. E. P. Dutton, 1974.

McCormick, Harold W., and Allen, Tom, *Shadows in the Sea: The Sharks, Skates and Rays*. Chilton Company, 1963.

Ommanney, F.D., *The Fishes*. Time-Life Books, 1970.

———, *The Ocean*. Oxford University Press, 1949.

*Ricciuti, Edward R., *Killers of the Seas*. The Macmillan Company, 1973.

Ricketts, E.F., and Calvin, Jack, *Between Pacific Tides*. Stanford University Press, 1968.

Russell, Findlay E., *Venomous Marine Animals*. TFH Publications, 1972.

Smith, C. Lavett, *The Hidden Sea*. The Viking Press, 1970.

Sweeney, James, *A Pictorial History of Sea Monsters*. Crown Publishers, Inc., 1972.

*Thorson, Gunnar, *Life in the Sea*. World University Library, McGraw-Hill, 1971.

*Voss, Gilbert L., *Oceanography*. Golden Press, Western Publishing Company, 1972.

*Zim, Herbert, and Shoemaker, Hurst H., *Fishes: A Guide to Fresh- and Salt-water Species*. Golden Press, Western Publishing Company, 1955.

Index